4

BOOK OF Oriental Carpets and Rugs

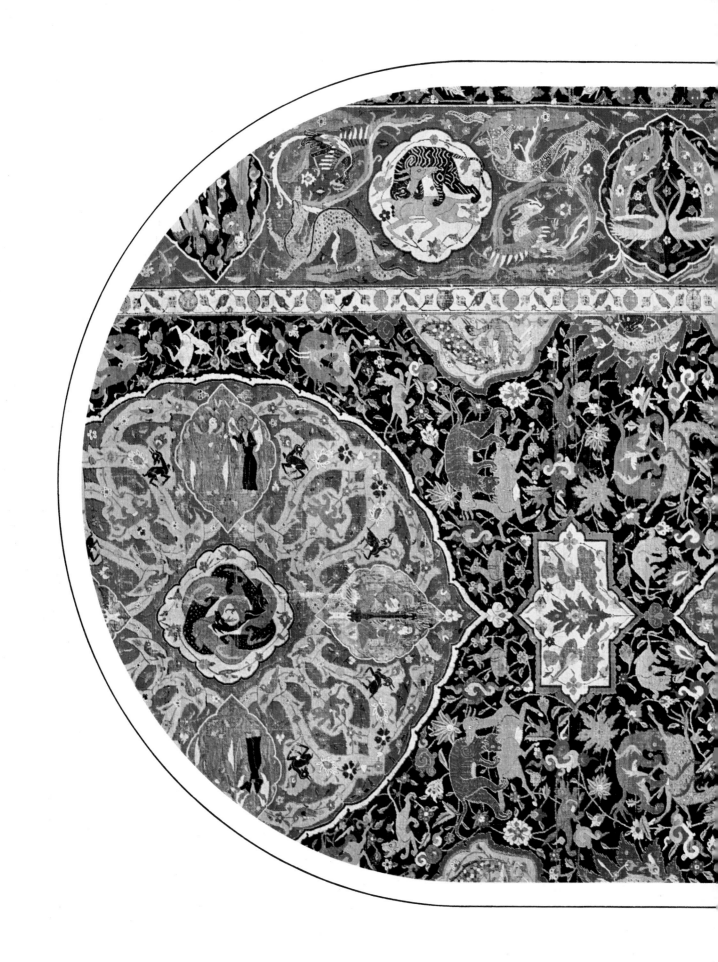

BOOK OF Oriental Carpets and Rugs

IAN BENNETT

HAMLYN

London · New York · Sydney · Toronto

published by
The Hamlyn Publishing Group Limited
London · New York · Sydney · Toronto
Hamlyn House, Feltham, Middlesex, England
© copyright The Hamlyn Publishing Group Limited 1972
ISBN 0 600 39249 X
Filmset in England by Filmtype Services Limited, Scarborough
Reproduced and printed in Spain
by Printer, Industria Gráfica sa, Tuset 19
Barcelona, San Vicente dels Horts, 1972
D. L. B. 27-72

For my mother

Frontispiece: Animal carpet (detail).
Persian, second half 16th century.
24 ft × 10 ft.
Made in a court manufactory of one of the Safavid
shahs, either Shah Abbas the Great or one of his
predecessors. The carpet shows remarkable skill in
the juxtaposition of colour, whereby the boldness
of the design is muted yet diversity is contained
within an overall unity. Animals, birds, flower-like
forms and arabesques are harmoniously combined
and reflect the Persian tradition, as in the
peacocks. Though Chinese influence can be seen in
the wavy cloud-bands, the carpet could only have
been made in Persia, and is a magnificent example
of the art of that country. Collection of Mr and Mrs
Louis E. Seley and family, New York, on loan to the
Metropolitan Museum of Art, New York.

Contents

Preface

Oriental carpets have attracted a small number of dedicated scholars and an equally small number of serious collectors. Yet many thousands of people own them. Most people are aware of the age and approximate value of paintings and furniture which they possess, but the coverings of floors somehow seem to be ignored.

On the other hand, many people have an exaggerated opinion of their carpet's importance, referring to it in awestruck tones as 'our Persian' or more commonly 'the Bokhara', a name which, in England at least, has become almost synonymous with Oriental carpets.

There has been in other words a distinctly laissez-faire attitude towards such things, and the object of this book is to try to demonstrate the richness and variety of Oriental carpets, and to analyse both the ways they are made and the enormous mass of ethnic, religious and geographical factors which cause one piece to be so different from (or so similar to) another.

Nevertheless, a word of warning: however cogent and useful a book may be in explaining a given subject, the reader is of necessity absorbing another's opinions, prejudices and possibly blindnesses. There can be no substitute for direct contact, for first-hand experience. There are many museums in England and America which have fine collections of Oriental carpets – those in the Victoria and Albert Museum, London, and the Metropolitan Museum, New York, are two of the greatest in the world – while most cities have dealers and auction houses which can be visited without, as the saying goes, obligation to buy.

The Somerset House Conference signed Pantaja de la Cruz. 1604. National Portrait Gallery, London.
Oriental carpets were so highly prized in Europe that they more often graced the table than the floor.

1 A General Introduction

No-one is exactly certain when weaving began. It was certainly in existence in Pharaonic Egypt and was probably known to the ancient Chinese. There are several biblical references. In Exodus XXXV. 35 we read: 'Them hath he filled with wisdom of heart, to work all manner of work, of the engraver, and of the cunning workman, and of the embroiderer, in blue, and in purple, in scarlet, and in fine linen, and of the weaver, even of them that do any work, and of those that devise cunning work.' The same chapter makes frequent references to wall hangings and altar cloths, although not, significantly perhaps, to floor coverings. The spear of Goliath is compared to the weaver's beam, whilst King Hezekiah moans, 'I have cut off like a weaver my life'. In Proverbs, a woman, 'with the attire of an harlot, and subtil of heart', says, 'I have decked my bed with coverings of tapestry', and Job, like Hezekiah, makes a powerful metaphor of transience when he says, 'my days are swifter than a weaver's shuttle'.

Numbers in the margin refer to the page where a coloured illustration may be found

Centres of carpet production

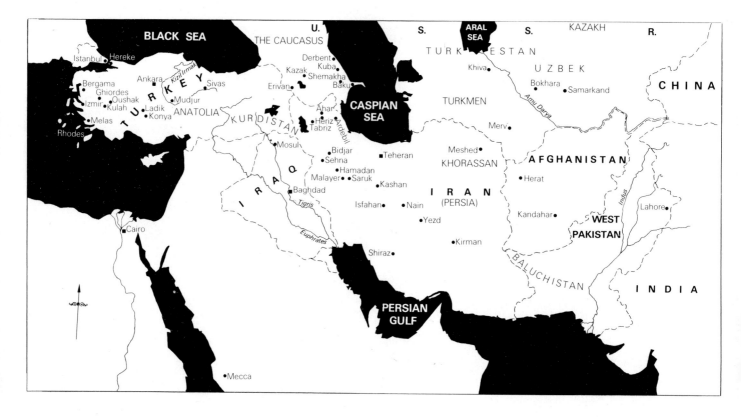

Such casual references as these, and others which may be found in Homer (purple carpets are mentioned in the *Iliad*) and later Classical authors, make it seem likely that even in these ancient times, 3000–2000 BC, weaving was already an established part of everyday life. Further evidence for this assumption comes from the Egyptian tomb of Mehenwetre, a royal steward who died *c.* 2000 BC; a fresco decorating the walls of his funeral chamber depicts many scenes of Egyptian life including women weaving flax.

Although we know of no hand-knotted carpets surviving from so early a period, a recent Russian archaeological expedition to the Altai mountains of southern Siberia has excavated a royal burial mound containing an almost miraculously preserved carpet. The Pazyryk carpet, as it is called, must date from *c.* 500 BC yet it is superbly designed and hand knotted, and is the equal of any piece produced in that area since. That such a piece could have been so beautifully made at such a time presupposes a long history of carpet-weaving in the Altai mountains, which abut on south-west Mongolia and north-west China.

To move on to more recent times, we know that carpet-weaving has been one of the most prized arts of the Middle and Far East for close on seven hundred years. What the newcomer to the subject finds remarkable is the longevity of both the methods and, more importantly, the designs. It is probably true to say that in no other field of the applied arts has it been possible for a type of object produced five hundred years or more ago to be still made today using the same techniques and in the same styles. As an aesthetic, stylistic phenomenon, Oriental carpets would appear to be unique. The designs used centuries ago are still used today and are made richer by the great tradition which lies behind them.

If over the centuries the styles of carpets have changed little, the people who made them have retained, in many cases, their traditional tribal ways of life, although political and social factors have caused their frequent and continuing migrations. As a result, the classification of Oriental carpets has many pitfalls. These pitfalls are usually most clearly seen by someone attempting to read a long book on the subject. Synonyms for various carpet-weaving centres appear to abound, and the generalisations made about a particular country or area seem to fall down for the majority of pieces discussed.

Persia, for instance (for simplicity we shall avoid using the modern name of Iran), is one of the six great carpet-producing areas, the others being Turkey, the

Life in the Camp by Mir Sayyid Ali. *c.* 1540.
Fogg Art Museum, Harvard University, Cambridge, Mass.
Gift of Joseph V. McMullan.
A Persian miniature painting showing a variety of carpets
in use as well as many of the flowers, animals and objects
which appear as carpet motifs.

The Pazyryk carpet.
The Hermitage Museum, Leningrad.
The earliest-known hand-knotted carpet,
about 2,500 years old.

Caucasus, Turkestan, India and China. Persian carpets in general use the Persian or Sehna knot and in terms of design are floral. Yet many pieces made in the north of the country, in areas adjacent to the Caucasian border where nomadic tribes have crossed and settled, are woven with a typical Caucasian geometricity. Two of the most famous of Persian carpet towns, Heriz and Shiraz, often produce very geometrically designed carpets; several other areas which have been partly settled by nomads originally of Turkish origin produce geometric patterns; whilst to add to the apparent confusion, a distant result of the Mongol invasions of the thirteenth century has been the introduction and continued use of certain Chinese motifs in Persian pieces.

Another problem, and this is mainly a scholarly one, is that there has been no obvious attempt to standardise the spellings of names. A quick glance at a cross-section of books on Oriental carpets will quickly demonstrate that the places spelt one way in one book are different in another and different yet again in a third. Names also appear and disappear and are even, in some cases, assigned to different countries.

The first thing the learner has to do is to make himself aware of the geographical areas with which he is dealing. The majority of carpets on the market today come from western Asia, the area we would perhaps describe as the Middle East. This area, with regard to carpets, is usually divided up as follows: Turkey, Persia, Afghanistan, the Caucasus, Turkestan and, in certain old books, Baluchistan. The first three need no explanation. The last three, however, do need some glossing.

The Caucasus, an area of roughly 166,500 square miles, is bounded on the west by the Black Sea and on the east by the Caspian and forms a link between Europe and Asia. An area rather than a country, it was part of Persia until the early nineteenth century when it was ceded to the jurisdiction of Imperial Russia. It is now part of the U.S.S.R. At no time, however, was it a particularly homogeneous area being a mixture of various races and peoples. Three of its most important regions are the Soviet States of Armenia (which was overrun by the Turks during the First World War), Azerbaijan and Georgia. There are many different types of carpet from the Caucasus which we will discuss in some detail later.

Turkestan is also an area now almost solely referred to in connection with carpets. The home of the ubiquitous Bokhara, the generic term for carpets woven in this district is Turkoman; today the area consists of the Soviet States of Turkmen, Uzbek and Kazakh, which

12

stretches to the borders of China. All in all, Turkestan is an area of close on three million square miles. Turkoman carpets, however, also come from northern Persia, Afghanistan and Pakistan, woven in those countries by nomadic tribes.

Finally Baluchistan: since 1947, the area known in old books by this name has been part of West Pakistan and is bordered by Persia on the west and Afghanistan on the north. Its old capital was the city of Kelat, although most of the carpets are marketed in the town of Bokhara in Uzbek as they have been for generations.

Because of the close associations of the nomadic Mohammedan tribes who inhabit what were once called Turkestan and Baluchistan, carpets from the latter place are very similar to Turkoman pieces and are usually classified with Turkoman carpets.

Knots

An important factor in deciding a carpet's origin is the recognition of the type of knot with which it is tied. Although this is never quite so easy as some authors would have us imagine, and although there are frequent exceptions to the general rules, knots are extremely useful guides.

There are basically two types: the Turkish knot, which is often called Ghiordes after the name of a carpet-weaving city in Turkey, and the Persian knot, which is sometimes called Sehna after the Persian town of that name. The bases of a carpet are two sets of threads: the fixed warp threads which run from north to south across which the weft threads are woven from east to west separating each row of knots. The difference between the two knots outlined above is that the Turkish (Ghiordes) is knotted around two warp threads whilst the Persian (Sehna) is knotted around one warp and looped under the next in an S pattern. Each knot is tied by hand, and in some of the very finest Persian carpets there can be anything between five hundred and a thousand knots to the square inch. In recent years, some carpets both from Persia and Turkey have been tied with what are known as jufti or false knots. These are tied in the same way as true knots but instead of one knot utilising two warp threads it utilises four. This obviously means that a carpet can be woven in half the time because there are half the number of knots, but it also has the effect of producing a coarse, loosely woven piece which will not wear nearly as well as a more densely knotted carpet.

In areas where carpet-weaving is the main industry, the skilful craftsman can tie about fifteen knots a minute

Medallion animal and floral carpet
with inscriptions.
Persian, 16th century.
Poldi Pezzoli Museum, Milan.
Most people's idea of a typical
Persian carpet.

Bergama carpet.
Turkish, early 19th century.
In contrast to the Persian
floral style, an extreme
example of Turkish geometricity.

14

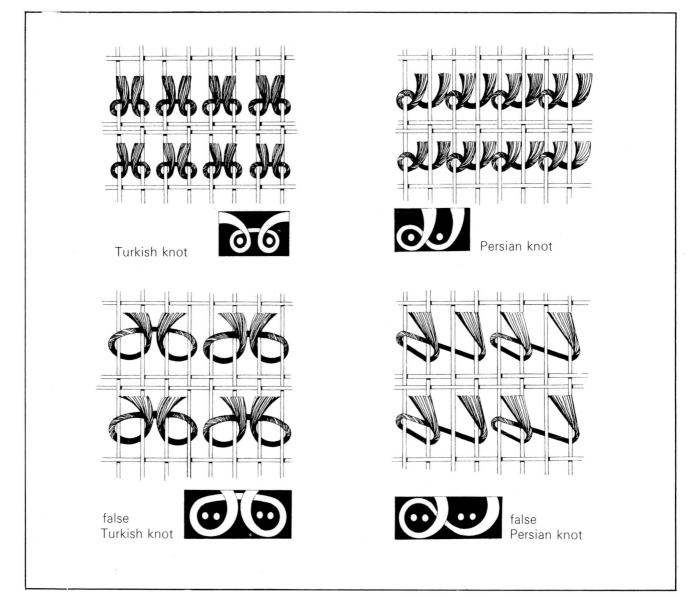

Turkish knot

Persian knot

false
Turkish knot

false
Persian knot

Diagram of knotting techniques

or around eight thousand a day. This means that it would take him just over two months to weave a carpet ten feet by six feet with a hundred knots to the square inch. On pieces this size or larger, however, more than one weaver will be employed, and on extra large carpets anything up to six weavers can be occupied at any one time. They work from a chart which shows them the number of knots to be tied in each colour and the colours to be used.

As to where the two kinds of knots are used, there are some general rules and many exceptions. The majority of Oriental carpets are tied with the Turkish knot; all Turkish and Caucasian pieces use it as do many Turkoman and quite a few Persian. Carpets tied with the Persian knot mainly come from Persia itself, although it is used in some Turkoman pieces as well as in those from Baluchistan and China.

In geographical terms the dividing line is the Caspian

Sea. West of it, the Turkish knot is used almost exclusively and to the east the Persian is predominant. Persia is either side of the dividing line so either knot may be used there. Indeed, it is an ironic fact that there are probably more types of carpet produced in Persia with the Turkish knot than with the Persian.

Materials

The material most frequently used in Oriental carpets is wool. After this, goat's hair, camel's hair, cotton and silk are also employed but to not nearly the same extent.

The best wool comes from the western part of Persia where it borders on Turkey. This is a region inhabited largely by Kurdish tribes and in older carpet books is often referred to as Kurdistan. The peerless quality of this wool is the obvious reason for the pre-eminence of Persian carpets.

Goat's hair is used mainly in Turkoman carpets where the soft, fine mohair of the angora goat is also used. Cashmere, from the Tibetan goat, is occasionally found in Indian, Chinese and of course Tibetan fabrics. Camel's hair, a tough and very durable material, is found in carpets from eastern Persia, Pakistan (old Baluchistan) and in those pieces called Mosul. This last name is in fact a trade name and has no known connection with the city of that name in Iraq, the carpets being made in western Persia and Turkey by Kurdish tribes and marketed in the town of Hamadan. This is yet another of those apparently inexplicable anomalies with which carpet lore abounds.

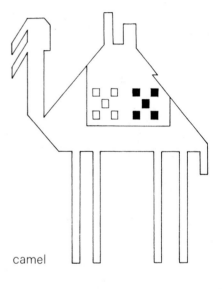

camel

Cotton is used extensively in Persian carpets to make the warp and weft threads. Although it is rarely used in the pile, certain Bokharas may occasionally have small areas of white woven in cotton.

It is likely that silk carpets first originated in China, since the silk-worm has been cultivated for countless centuries in that country. It was also considered a material denoting wealth and luxury as indeed it does today and was generally only used for carpets woven for Holy Places, for prayer rugs and for royalty, who were the only people who could afford to supply a weaver with the quantities necessary.

Antique silk pieces are therefore rare, although such carpets are not in any case particularly practical as silk is not a material which wears well. During the present century, a poor quality commercial variety has been produced with a pile running in the wrong direction (towards the top). They are almost always made in the city of Caesarea.

The material used in the warp and weft threads can

The Ardebil Mosque carpet (detail).
Persian, first half 16th century.
34 ft × 17 ft 6 in. Victoria and Albert Museum, London.
The cartouche with inscription and date may be seen at the top.
Probably the finest carpet in the world.

Austrian royal hunting carpet (detail).
Persian, 16th century.
22 ft 4 in × 10 ft 6 in.
Österreichisches Museum für angewandte
Kunst, Vienna.
There are close links between the figures
in the carpet and those in Persian
miniature painting (see page 11).

often be of some help in determining the particular area from which a given carpet derives. The majority of Persian pieces have cotton for both the warp and weft, although there are important exceptions. Shiraz pieces for instance if they are antique always have wool, and modern examples have a cotton warp and wool weft. Wool was always used in Niris carpets, and occasionally in those from Herat, Khorassan and Tabriz. Kirmans usually have a wool weft, whilst those made by Kurds are usually woven with wool throughout.

Wool is generally used for the warp and weft for carpets from most of the other major weaving centres although from Turkey the Ghiordes occasionally has a warp of either linen or silk, whilst the Kulah not infrequently has a cotton weft. Some Caucasian carpets, such as the Derbends and Shirvans, have a cotton warp and weft whilst a few Turkoman pieces, mainly the Yomuds and Afghans (these last also from Afghanistan), may employ goat's hair.

A modern type, which although not woven is worth mentioning is the felt rug, a Persian product made in the

Detail of a kilim showing weft-face technique.

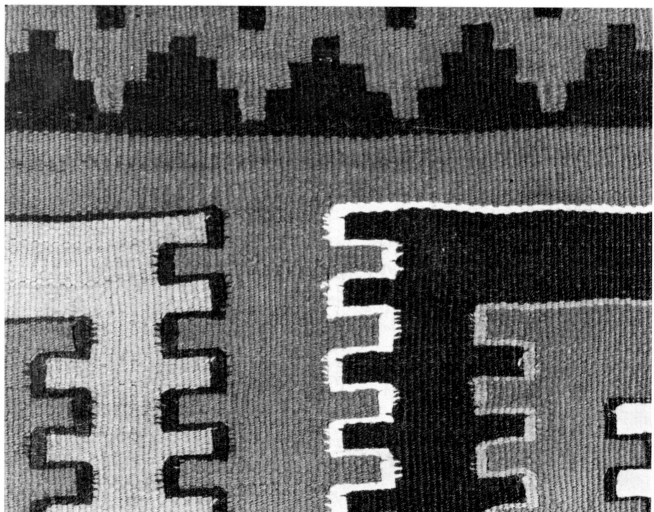

three cities of Yezd, Astrabad and Isfahan. Such pieces can be made from any one of the types of hair mentioned above or a combination of two or more of them. The hair is soaked and pounded until a flat, thick and durable small carpet results. They are not dyed but retain the natural colour of the hair used: white, grey or brown. They are employed in the East as floor coverings over which woven carpets are placed, a practice which has given rise in the West to the use of under-felt.

119 Finally there are the kilims. These are weft-face carpets woven like tapestries, without a knotted pile. The patterns are made from the coloured weft threads which are visible on both sides of the piece. Kilims are woven in all parts of the Middle East and although not as attractive as pile carpets, are nevertheless hard wearing and have their own charm. The finest type is the Sehna kilim which follows Sehna knotted carpets in design. The Anatolian and Kurdish kilims usually consist of two (the Anatolian) or more strips woven together, whilst the Shirvan kilim is unusual in having diagonal bands of colour upon which are woven geometric designs similar to those found on Daghestan carpets. Merv kilims are also distinctive in that the bands of embroidered zig-zag colours run diagonally across the carpet instead of vertically or horizontally. The best kilims, which were used in the Orient as floor coverings, are antique pieces although some very good ones are being woven today in Turkey.

Some Famous Carpets

Unquestionably the most famous group of carpets are those from the Mosque at Ardebil in Persia, the most
18 important of which is the Ardebil Mosque carpet in the Victoria and Albert Museum, London, which scholars have for many years shown an unusual unanimity in accepting as the greatest example of carpet weaving in the world! It has a silk warp and weft and a wool pile; the Persian knot is used with approximately 350 knots to the square inch, making an incredible thirty-two million knots in all. It bears the inscription: 'I have no refuge in the world other than thy threshold. There is no place of protection for my head other than this door. The work of the slave of the Threshold Maqsud the slave of the Holy Place of Kashan in the year 946.' The date 946 refers to the Mohammedan year and is equivalent to 1540. The two other carpets from the same source are the magnificent hunting carpet in the Metropolitan Museum, New York, which has four hundred knots to the square inch, and the Baker hunting carpet which has about five hundred knots to the square inch.

The Chelsea carpet (detail).
Persian, early 16th century.
17 ft 8 in × 9 ft 8 in.
Victoria and Albert Museum, London.
The freedom and imagination
shown in the decoration make this
an outstanding piece.

Moghul hunting carpet.
Indian, late 16th or early 17th century. 8 ft × 5 ft 1 in.
Museum of Fine Arts, Boston.
Gift of Mrs Frederick L. Ames in the name of Frederick L. Ames.
The pictorial style is typical of carpets from Moghul India.

We have already discussed the amazingly preserved royal carpet from Altai in Russia known as the Pazyryk carpet; another famous carpet, although nearly two thousand years later in date, is the Dragon and the Phoenix carpet in the Staatliche Museem, Berlin, probably woven in the Caucasus in the fourteenth century. This is a carpet of great art historical importance. In the Spedale di Santa Maria della Scala, Siena, there is a series of frescoes by the Italian painter Domenico di Bartolo; one of these frescoes depicts the *Marriage of the Foundlings* in which a carpet very similar to the Dragon and the Phoenix is portrayed. By a strange coincidence this carpet was purchased by the German museum from an Italian church early in this century.

Amongst other great pieces which anyone interested in carpets should try and see is the Austrian royal hunting carpet which is said to have been presented to the Imperial Austro-Hungarian court by Peter the Great. This is now in the Österreichisches Museum für angewandte Kunst, Vienna. Made in Persia in the middle of the sixteenth century it is probably the greatest hunting carpet in the world and may have been made, like the Ardebil pieces, either at Isfahan or possibly at Kashan. It is woven throughout in silk; the Persian knot is used with 783 knots to the square inch. On its deep crimson ground are depicted an assortment of animals of the chase, including deer, wolves, lions and leopards.

The Boston Museum of Fine Arts possesses a splendid Moghul hunting carpet made in India in the late sixteenth or early seventeenth century and has 372 knots to the square inch. The magnificent Altman prayer rug, named after the great American collector Benjamin Altman who donated it to the Metropolitan Museum, was woven with a silk pile in Persia about 1580 during the Safavid period.

The early sixteenth-century Persian animal carpet in the Victoria and Albert Museum, known as the Chelsea carpet, has a silk warp and weft, a wool pile with 470 knots to the square inch and is one of the greatest pieces of its kind. Also in London is the John Bell Indo-Isfahan carpet, woven at the Moghul Imperial workshops at Lahore around 1620, one of six pieces of this kind which were brought into England soon after they were made. This carpet is on view at the Girdlers Hall in the City of London.

24

2 Dyes, Colours, Designs

26, 27 The first sight of a fine old Oriental carpet gives one the impression of tremendous richness and variety of design combined with a superb and immensely subtle use of colour. The more modern a carpet, however, the more often one notices with a sense of regret that the influence of the tremendous Western demand for Oriental pieces combined with the new synthetic dyes have caused an obvious decline in the quality of most products.

Carpets are usually classified in three age groups. Antiques can be anything from fifty to 450 years old, although hardly anything dating from before 1600 comes on the market and very little from before 1700. A definition of antique carpets, which may also apply to semi-antiques has been given by the great authority on Persian art, Arthur Upham Pope: 'ignoring dates we can say that an antique rug is one that has not been chemically washed, that has an unrestored pile [this is not necessarily true] and was woven according to local methods and designs before the latter was extensively modified by European influence.'

The second grouping is known as semi-antique and refers to carpets between ten and fifty years old, whilst the third is known as modern and refers to the new pieces made for export which are to be found in dealers showrooms for retail sale in the usual way.

The factors which go towards making one carpet more valuable than another are easily stated: the fineness of the weave, the quality of the materials used, the richness of the dyes, the diversity and imaginativeness of the design, the condition of the piece, and of course its age.

Dyes

Of all these points the one to be most carefully marked is dye. Almost all Oriental carpets made before 1900 employed the traditional types of dye used for centuries, those derived from natural products and known as vegetable dyes. By the end of the nineteenth century the

Kuba carpet (detail).
Caucasian, 17th century.
Designs of more modern carpets
are often modified by
Western influence.

Herat carpet.
Persian, early 17th century.
The colours are rich and subtle, as to be
expected in an antique piece.

demand for carpets in the West had become so great that synthetic dyes, developed in Europe and America, were imported into Persia, Turkey and other Eastern countries to help speed up carpet production.

Such dyes were introduced around 1870–1880. Until the end of the First World War, the traditional dyeing methods, while steadily declining from use, were at least employed sufficiently widely to ensure that many superb pieces were produced. From 1920, however, vegetable dyes virtually ceased to be used and there are now only a very small number of carpets being made with them.

The effect this has had on the quality of modern carpets has been drastic. The most important advantage of vegetable over synthetic dyes is that the former do not fade, they mellow; the latter not only fade, they also fade at different rates, depending upon the different colours used in a carpet, and in some cases they change their original colour completely. Pieces which have been dyed naturally therefore grow more beautiful with age, whilst pieces dyed synthetically progressively deteriorate.

It is fairly easy, even for a beginner, to detect the difference between vegetable and synthetic dyes. One of the most obvious differences can be seen on a large plain field of a single colour, blue or red for instance. In a vegetable-dyed piece, the wool will have been dipped at different times and faint stripes of differing shades, known as abrash, show on the finished product.

Synthetically dyed pieces will generally not show such stripes, although the manufacturers of modern pieces have taken to introducing them artificially in order to confuse purchasers. A further test, therefore, is to separate the pile and examine the colour of the wool near the knot. Because synthetic dyes tend to change colour, the wool deep in the carpet will often be a different colour to that on the surface. This is particularly true of composite colours where one has been mixed with another to make a third. A yellow surface may, when the deep pile is examined carefully, turn out to have been at one stage green, the blue having entirely disappeared through exposure to light. In the vegetable-dyed piece the surface and the deep pile will be green, although of slightly differing shades.

Like bronzes and silver, fine old carpets will also in time take on a surface sheen known as a patina due to the continual polishing of the surface by its contact with feet. Again, wily modern manufacturers have faked a sheen by chemical processes, by either bathing the carpets in a specially prepared solution or coating them with a substance like glycerine and then rolling them between

meander

Greek key

latch hook

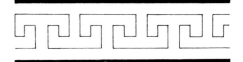

T border

zig-zag

hot rollers. However, a sheen thus artificially induced will not last and indeed may often cause the fibres to rot.

Thus the would-be purchaser of an Oriental carpet should bear several things in mind. Any carpet made this century is likely to be synthetically dyed and will not improve with age. Pre-1900 vegetable-dyed pieces will, on the other hand, improve with age if carefully treated. Carpets, like any other fine work of art, should not only give the purchaser many years of pleasurable ownership but should also, if and when they are sold, realise a substantial profit on the purchase price. The chances of a synthetically dyed piece increasing in value, however, are minimal.

Natural dyes are with one exception all derived from plants or insects. The exception is black. This colour is made by soaking iron shavings in vinegar. The result is an acid substance which is the only natural dye to have a corrosive effect on wool. Brown, which is usually obtained by mixing madder and yellow, but is also obtained from valonia, gall-nuts and green walnut shells, does not have a particularly long-lasting effect and has a tendency to dull with age. The most successful colours, and the ones which tend to be used most frequently, are the blues, yellows and reds. Yellow, as well as dark green, is extensively used in Persian carpets. Red is the favourite colour of Turkish and Turkestan dyers whilst blue is found on many Caucasian, especially Armenian, fabrics.

Red, perhaps the most widely used of all colours, was obtained from three main sources and the shades of red can vary enormously. The most ancient source is from an insect called kermes, which lives in the bark of oak trees. They were collected in the summer and killed by the fumes of heated vinegar, a process which gives off acetic acid. The result is a deep, rich red which is probably the most permanent of all natural dyes.

Cochineal, the insect found on cacti in Mexico, gives a carmine red and has only been introduced into the East in comparatively recent times. The dye is obtained by crushing large quantities of the female insect, and has largely surplanted kermes in the dying of carpets. Cochineal was often combined with other things to give different colours such as purple when combined with bichromate of potash, cherry or pink with madder, and scarlet with sulphuric acid.

The third main source of red was the madder root which was boiled and then pounded. It gave many different shades and was most frequently used mixed with other substances such as alum or with a mixture of milk, fermented grape juice and water which gave violet.

Chinese runner (detail).
Early 19th century.
The colours and motifs are
typical of Chinese pieces.

Antique animal and floral carpet (detail). Persian.
Österreichisches Museum für angewandte Kunst, Vienna.
Note the inner border with the decorative script.

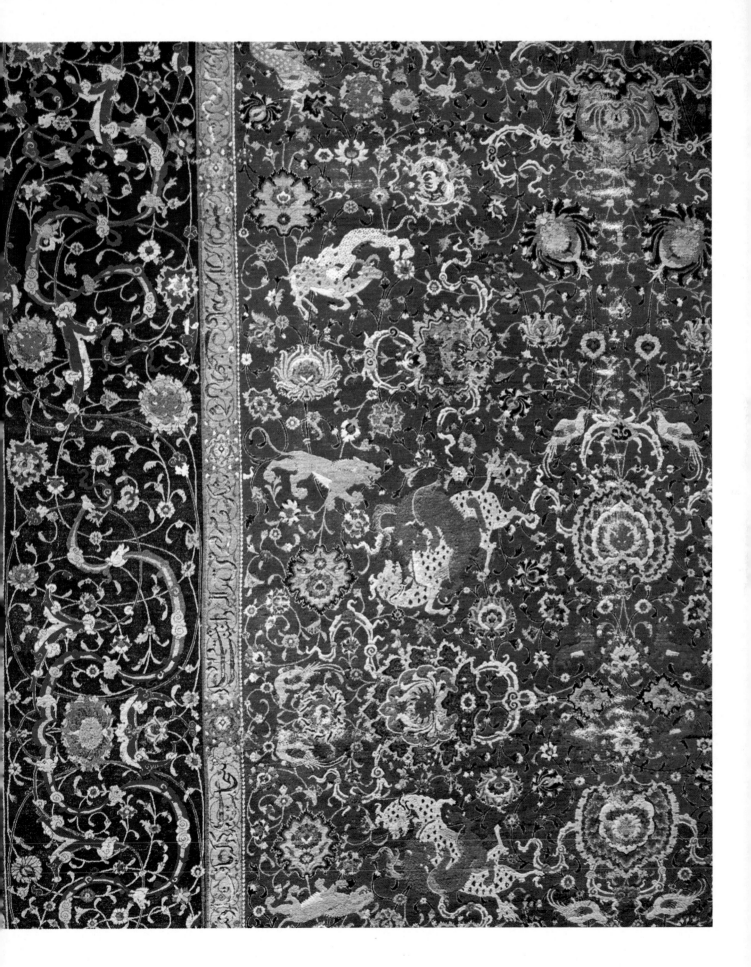

Towards the end of the period when vegetable dyes were widely used, dye woods such as campeachy and Brazil wood were almost always employed together with an assortment of vegetation: onions, beetroot, ivy etc. The results were cheaper dyes which were not nearly so fine. Blue was obtained largely from the leaves of the indigofera plant, cultivated in India, which were dissolved in sulphuric acid to which alum had been added. Persian blue, a deep rich shade, was the result of dying indigo over madder. Yellow and indigo also gave green.

Yellow, like red, was obtained from various sources the main ones being Persian berries, turmeric, saffron and sumach roots. Persian berries gave a long lasting but dull colour whilst turmeric gave a bright orange (as does pomegranate peel). A light yellow was obtained from larkspur and a greenish yellow from the fungus of the mulberry bush. The vivid, rich yellow of saffron, extracted from the stamen of the Mediterranean crocus, was always and still is one of the most valued of substances. Towards the end of the nineteenth century, a dull, buff yellow was obtained from the bark of the quercitron tree.

octagons

Amongst the other colours often met with are grey, obtained from Smyrna nuts mixed with copperas, and purple. Although normally obtained from existing colour combinations, such as mixing various reds with indigo to give shades of purple, heliotrope and lavender, purple can also be obtained from molluscs and other marine creatures. It is well known that the ancient Phoenicians produced a wonderfully vivid purple dye from shellfish found in the Aegean and that this became the colour of Imperial Rome and has for ever afterwards been associated with royalty. Unfortunately, like Stradivari's varnish, the secret of this substance has been lost. All the foregoing is part of the past. The amount of vegetable dye found in carpets today is minimal.

The older form of synthetic dye is largely a substance derived from coal and is called aniline. Although the various carpet-producing countries originally attempted to forbid the use of aniline dyes (in Persia a dyer found using them had his right hand chopped off), their obvious short-term advantages and the economic benefits resulting therefrom outweighed the aesthetic considerations.

Although over short periods, aniline dyes appear to be able to withstand the effects of light, heat and air more than vegetable products, this ability is not lasting. Not only do they fade and change colour over long periods but they also have the disastrous effect of drying the fibres making them brittle and fragile. After a few years, therefore, an aniline-dyed piece can be in a bad state.

Colours

Colours in Oriental Carpets are not only used for decoration. It should be remembered that the peoples of Middle Eastern countries, whatever their religion, are generally extremely devout. Thus colours have important symbolic values, as indeed they used to have in medieval Europe.

White is an almost pan-Eastern symbol of mourning; it has this significance in Persia, China and India and is thus symbolic to Mohammedans. Because of its association with death, it can also mean peace. The same significance may attach to sky blue which is also the national colour of Persia. Green is the colour sacred to Mohammedans. It is the colour of life and signifies immortality. As such, it is rarely found in Turkish carpets, excepting prayer rugs, and it was only around 1930 that it began to be found on Turkish fabrics to any great extent. The colour green has always been used freely by non-Islamic peoples.

Black is a universal symbol of sorrow, evil and destruction, and it is rarely found. In contrast, red means joy, life and all the goodly virtues and is therefore, not surprisingly, the most widely used colour. The 'power' colours are gold (not to be confused with orange, which is a Buddhist and Mohammedan colour for sorrow), purple which is, as it has been since Classical times, the imperial colour, Moghul blue and yellow, which, like gold, is a Chinese royal colour. Indigo blue signifies solitude. Rose or pink means divine wisdom, whilst brown, the colour of earth, signifies fertility.

Any carpet, therefore, is not just a beautiful design utilising floral or geometric motifs but, even if a representational type, is in essence an abstraction. Not only the colours but also the patterns often have deep religious and emotional meanings which are lost on the uninitiated. The same is true, as we have said before, of European medieval art and literature where colours and animals often acted as the writing between the lines, the symbolism which directed the educated beholder to the real significance of the work of art.

Designs

In his famous book on carpets *The Practical Book of Oriental Rugs* first published in 1911, Dr G. Griffin Lewis describes how certain patterns and colours were used exclusively by individual tribes and even by individual families. Thus, by a process of deduction, an expert should be able to tell at least the district if not the exact village where an antique carpet was woven. In practice, however, one has to take into account that in modern

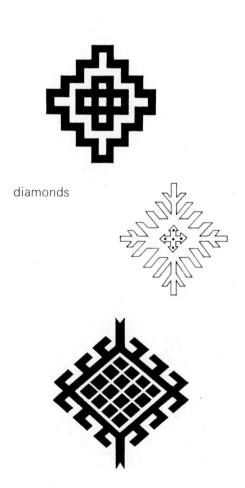

diamonds

Hunting carpet (detail).
Persian, 16th century.
Poldi Pezzoli Museum, Milan.
Here is a multitude of animal
and floral motifs.

Large Kurdistan garden carpet (detail).
Persian, 18th century. 27 ft × 8 ft 9 in.
The field shows stylised insects and trees, while the border
has the latch-look motif.
The designs of Kurdistan carpets have a geometricity which is
uncharacteristic of Persian pieces, and is due to the proximity of
Turkey and the Caucasus.

times war, immigration and travel have tended to cause a severe blow to such distinctions, although there are enough pieces being produced utilising traditional designs to make the generalisation still valid.

In broad terms, the various major carpet-weaving areas can be divided into those which use floral designs and those which use geometric shapes and patterns. The floral countries are Persia and India, Turkey is a mixture of both floral and geometric with the latter predominant, whilst Caucasian and Turkoman pieces are almost always geometric; on the few occasions when floral designs are used these become stylised and rectilinear. Chinese carpets are in a special class of their own. It is probably true to say that although the beginner could confuse any number of, to the expert, widely differing carpet designs, he will always be able to tell the Chinese piece. Dragons, monsters and an abundance of that distinctive pattern known descriptively as cloud-band are regularly found on such carpets.

On antique Turkish carpets, it is extremely unusual to find any living creature, either animal or human, woven into the design. Even though there is nothing in the Koran which specifically forbids the representation of living forms, many of the Prophet's sayings have been interpreted by Orthodox Mohammedans as a prohibition against figural images in works of art (although the extent of the prohibition seems to vary).

Many older pieces, especially prayer rugs, carry inscriptions woven into the margin. These are usually quotations from the Koran, although it is not unusual to find short stanzas or lines from some of the better-known Persian poets. Carpets are rarely signed, one famous exception being the Ardebil Mosque carpet, although many are dated. Just as the Christian calendar begins with the birth of Christ, so the Mohammedan calendar begins on 16th July 622, the day the Prophet set out on his journey from the Holy City of Mecca to the Holy City of Medina. It should also be remembered that the Mohammedan year is shorter than ours and gains one day in every 33·7 years. A quick method of finding out the approximate equivalent to the Western date is to add 583. Thus a rug dated say 1236 in the Mohammedan calendar will be 1236 plus 583, equalling 1819. For a more exact date, divide the Mohammedan year by 33·7, subtract the result and then add 622, thus 1236 becomes 1821.

Animals, insects and birds are often featured in the designs of Oriental carpets. They can be highly stylised, or strikingly realistic like the wild animals on Persian hunting carpets. The following is a list of animals and

14
15
106, 114
30
31
18
34
19, 35

cloud-bands

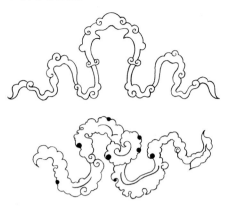

Arabic numerals

١ ٢ ٣ ٤ ٥ ٦ ٧ ٨ ٩ ٠
1 2 3 4 5 6 7 8 9 0

birds most frequently found: bat, bee, beetle, boar, butterfly, camel, crab, crow, deer, dog, dove, dragon, duck, elephant, fly, hog, lion, magpie, parrot, peacock, phoenix, rooster, scorpion, sparrow, squirrel, stork, tarantula, tiger and tortoise.

As with colours, most of these creatures have a symbolic value above and beyond their mere decorative presence.

The scorpion and the tarantula denote viciousness and poison, and also represent defence. They are most frequently found in the borders of Caucasian pieces, especially those from Shirvan, Kazak and Kabistan, it being said that their continued presence beneath the feet teaches children to be unafraid and therefore lessens the risk of them being stung by attempting to shirk away from a live example; the tarantula pattern tends to be highly formalised.

Amongst the other creatures listed above, the camel denotes wealth and happiness. This is a logical symbol since not only is it the invaluable transport of desert nomads but it stores up water, is revered by all the desert peoples and when killed is a source of food and drink whilst its skin gives hair for weaving and also leather. The crab appears to have no symbolic significance, although it is, of course, one of the great astrological signs. It is doubtful whether the stylised ornament so often found in the borders of Caucasian, especially Kazak, carpets, is in fact a representation of this creature, but it is taken as such by most authorities. The faithful dog is sacred to Mohammedans as a talisman against robbers, spells and diseases.

Three universal power symbols are the elephant, the dragon and the lion. The elephant is a symbol of royalty in India. The dragon symbolises evil in Persia and death in India, but is revered in China where it has strong associations with Confucianism and also represents imperial power. The lion is an almost universal metaphor for authority, strength and in some countries such as India, royalty. Where fighting animals are shown on Oriental carpets, this symbolises the eternal struggle between good and evil.

2–3

Amongst Chinese symbols, the bat represents happiness, and the bee immortality through one's descendants, whilst the beetle (the Egyptian scarab) denotes creation and is the Chinese equivalent of the Islamic colour green (in India, the scarab is one of the symbols of royalty and power). The butterfly is a sign of vanity and is often met with in the borders of Chinese carpets, whilst the crow is a sign of bad luck not only for the Chinese but also for the

scorpion

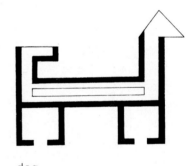

tarantula

dog

dragon

Rose ground vase carpet (detail).
Persian, late 16th or early 17th century.
Victoria and Albert Museum, London.

Moghul carpet.
Indian, 17th century.
Note the herati border and the carnations,
irises and lilies on the field.

Hindus; as is the case with a number of these symbols, however, it has exactly the opposite meaning for the Mohammedans.

The dove in China, as in most other world mythologies, denotes peace and companionship, whilst the duck is a symbol of a happy and faithful marriage. These contrast with the fly which to the Chinese signifies worthlessness, and the hog which denotes vice and madness (not to be confused with the Indian boar which, when shown with a sphere balanced on its right tusk, signifies the third incarnation of Vishnu when the God saved the world from the deluge).

The peacock which denotes royalty in India symbolises beauty in China, whilst the phoenix is the Chinese symbol of wealth and a rich bride. The tortoise, perhaps because of its own slowness and exceedingly long life-span, naturally denotes longevity and immortality as does the deer (to the Hindu, the tortoise is sacred as the symbol of the second incarnation of the Vishnu when the God supported the world on his back).

The parrot is the Indian equivalent of Eros, the messenger of life, and is often found on carpets as well as in Indian miniatures, where it is usually seen perching in the vicinity of a diaphanously robed recumbent lady. The rooster, in contrast, symbolises the devil for the people of Shiraz and is found on their carpets as a charm against evil. This pattern again is extremely formalised and can quite easily be confused with the pear or cone patterns which we will discuss later. The magpie symbolises good luck.

Two other birds, the sparrow and the stork, have widely differing meanings. The sparrow is found on Indian carpets and denotes fertility and a full harvest whilst the stork, a Chinese symbol of longevity, is an Indian symbol for dishonesty. Finally the squirrel; this is a symbol of the seventh incarnation of Vishnu and is therefore sacred to Hindus, signifying as it does the God's protection.

We can now move on from animals to flowers and fruit. The most important and recurring symbols are trees – cypress, palm, coconut-palm and willow. Whenever a tree is seen on a carpet it always has a deep religious significance and invariably symbolises the tree of life. It signifies immortality in the after-life and divine power. Certain trees, however, have an added meaning; thus the cypress, aptly known in the West as the 'sad' tree, is a powerful symbol of mourning but also has the meaning of heavenly immortality through death.

The same meaning attaches to the weeping willow amongst the Chinese. By contrast the palm and the

bird

parrot

coconut-palm are logical metaphors of fulfilment and blessing. Like the camel, these trees have a great significance for desert peoples since their presence implies water whilst the tree itself is a supplier of food. The same beneficient meaning attaches to the pomegranate.

Amongst other plants to which a special significance may attach are the pear, the peony and the lotus. The peony is frequently found on Chinese carpets and denotes wealth whilst the lotus to the Chinese foretells a great lineage and is sacred to the Buddhists of both China and India. The pear, one of the most common designs on Persian and Caucasian carpets, has proved a difficult symbol to interpret and there are a number of suggestions for its origin. This diversity of opinion is best demonstrated by the various names it has been called by different authorities: the boteh, the flame, the fir cone, the crown jewel, the seal, the almond nut, the palm leaf, the river bend, the feather and the bouquet.

The origins of these names are almost as extraordinary as the names themselves. The river bend, for instance, is suggested since the shape of the pattern bears a fanciful resemblance to the loop made by the river Indus on the plains of Upper Cashmere as seen from the mosque. The seal supporters contend that we are dealing with a formalised version of the shape made when a closed fist is dipped in blood and pressed upon a piece of paper, an ancient Eastern way of sealing official documents. The palm leaf would presumably have the same significance as the palm tree, although some would add that it is also the Greek sign of victory. The crown jewel theory arose because of the pear's resemblance to the great diamond in the Persian crown.

For Western readers, the closest description in words one can give is that the pear design was the origin for that apparently most traditional of English designs, the Paisley pattern. Large pears are found on carpets from the Caucasus and southern Persia, whilst on pieces from central and western Persia they are usually small. On Saraband and Shiraz carpets, the whole field is frequently taken up with the design, the pear being arranged in rows, with each alternate row having the stem turned in the opposite direction from the preceding one. Herats, Khorassans and Sehnas also use it as a main design although the stems in these examples are usually parallel.

So much for individual plants which have a special symbolism. There are others which do not appear to denote anything special but are often combined to produce a purely decorative scheme. The most common of these is probably the Shah Abbas design named after

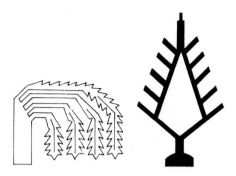

weeping willow and cypress

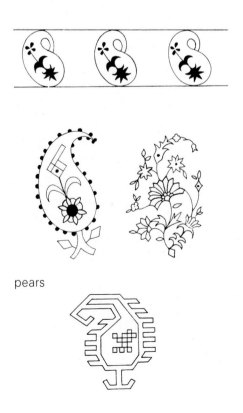

pears

Ladik prayer rug.
Turkish, early 18th century.
Compare the panelled mihrab
with the carpet below

Ghiordes prayer rug.
Turkish, late 18th century.
A mosque lamp hangs in the mihrab.

the great Persian king who reigned from 1586 to 1628. This consists of a central flower, which some authorities think was once meant to represent the pineapple, surrounded by a floral wreath. The wreath usually consists of yellow, red and blue flowers and the whole design is most frequently woven upon a blue or deep red background.

Another common design is the rosette which probably represents the Persian spring flower the star of Bethlehem, although the lotus has been suggested. It is used in alternation with a closed bud to form the knop-and-flower pattern commonly found in the borders of Persian fabrics. In nineteenth-century fabrics, the Sadar pattern, named after a governor of Azerbaijan called Sadar Aziz Khan, is found consisting of leaf shapes connected by vines and floral patterns.

The herati design is also one of the most prominent of Persian patterns and is sometimes known as the fish or twin-fish design. It is thought to have been first used in the city of Herat and consists of a rosette between two serrated leaves, which do in fact closely resemble fish. Common on Herat, Khorassan, Feraghan and Sehna fabrics, it is probably more used than any other design from this region. The so-called gul Henna design, as its name implies, consists of the small yellow henna flower arranged in rows and connected by a complicated floral pattern.

A Kurdish design is the mina khan, named after a ruler of western Persia, which is the area of the country largely populated by this once warlike people. Geometric green vines connect a lattice arrangement of red, yellow and blue floral bouquets. Finally, we should mention the lily, which on Turkish fabrics resembles a three-leaf clover and which is invariably found on Konya carpets, Konya being a synonym for the design; quatrefoil roses which on Kurdish fabrics may represent the tree of life; and the grain-of-rice pattern, small pinkish dots on a white field, which may be found on Chinese carpets and on those from Samarkand.

There are many other patterns or objects which have a religious or symbolic significance. Amongst the most common are baskets, beads, clouds, combs, conch shells, crescents, crosses (including the hooked cross or swastika), diamonds, eggs, hour glasses, endless knots, mountains, mihrabs (prayer niches), hanging lamps, octagons, window panels, and various kinds of stars.

Amongst all these, probably the various kinds of crosses are the most popular. The Greek or square cross is a Christian symbol and most Eastern Orthodox

mina khani

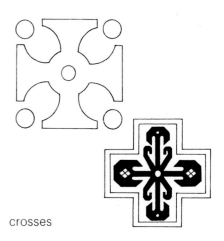

crosses

58, 59

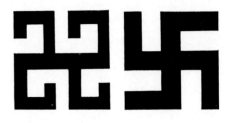

swastikas

churches are built in this shape; as such it is obviously not found on carpets woven by Mohammedan peoples. The swastika, however, is one of those strange universal symbols found in South America, Egypt, the Middle East, and India. Indeed, wherever a civilisation grew up it soon appeared, usually as a metaphor for the sun. Derived from the ancient Sanskrit word svasti, meaning honour, it is found together with simplified versions such as the latch hook (also known as the running-dog motif) on almost all Caucasian carpets, often as a border design, and on many other western Asian fabrics. In China it symbolises peace and privacy, a meaning which appears to have been forgotten in twentieth-century Europe.

The most frequent Mohammedan symbols are the crescent which signifies faith and is the symbol of Islam (in India it is associated with battle); the mihrab, or prayer niche, which is found on all prayer rugs, is pointed towards Mecca when prayed upon by the Faithful and is supposed to represent the alcove in the Great Mosque at Mecca; the hanging lamp, which is usually found at the arched end of the mihrab on Turkish prayer rugs, especially those from Konya, Ladik and Ghiordes; and the panel shapes which are meant to represent Mosque windows and are most commonly found on Shirazes.

43
42

Other designs with Islamic attributes are prayer beads, found on prayer rugs, and combs. As in the Roman Catholic religion, every Mohammedan has a rosary. In ancient times such an object, being circular and therefore endless, was a natural symbol of immortality, and, like the circular prayer wheel of the Buddhists, may have logically lent itself to later religious observance. The Mohammedan rosary has ninety-nine beads, each one of them standing for a divine name of Allah. The comb, another object frequently woven in the prayer rugs, is illustrative of the strictly observed Islamic belief (the faithful comb their hair before praying) that 'cleanliness is next to Godliness'.

102

endless knot

Another almost universal talisman is the endless knot, called in Chinese ch'ang, a symbol of wisdom and immortality. Readers of the middle-English romance *Sir Gawain and the Green Knight* will recall that the hero had such a knot upon his shield, as did King Arthur himself, as a defence against harm. It also fascinated Renaissance draughtsmen like Dürer, Raphael and Leonardo.

Various types of stars are frequently found on Caucasian and Turkoman carpets. The form which resembles a star and a cross combined, with each of the four arms terminating in two points, is probably an unconscious adaptation of the Christian symbol. An eight-pointed

Tabriz carpet (detail).
Persian, first half 16th century.
Musée des Arts Décoratifs, Paris.
Flowers, birds, trees, a waterfall and
mythical beasts make a
rhythmical pattern.

'Star Oushak' carpet.
Turkish, c. 1600.
14 ft 7 in × 7 ft 7 in.
Metropolitan Museum of Art, New York.
Gift of Joseph V. McMullan 1958.

star, the centre in the form of a square, is often found in an octagon and is taken by old authorities to be a symbol for the ancient God of the Medes, one-time rulers of Persia. The octagon itself, which is frequently found on Chinese, Caucasian and, predominantly, Turkoman fabrics, is a compass symbol signifying the universe.

Finally, there is the familiar six-pointed star of David, the symbol of the Jewish faith which has spread throughout the whole of the East. It is probable that all stars were originally revered as messengers of the Gods and as guides, not only physically but also astrologically.

Amongst Buddhist symbols frequently found on Chinese carpets but also on Middle Eastern fabrics, presumably having found their way there through the Mongol invasions, are the bow knot, emblem of the Buddha himself, the basket, signifying plenty, the conch shell and the Chinese fret, almost a hallmark of Chinese carpets and signifying the Divine Abode of Ursa Major and immortality. The pole medallion probably originated in China and evolved from a highly formalised representation of a lotus; it is found on many of the most important types of Persian carpet. A Moghul symbol, the mountain peak, the abode of the souls of the dead, is also found on some Middle Eastern fabrics, although as with all symbols from the Far East any symbolic significance is probably unintended as they move west.

The egg is a logical Chinese symbol of fertility; the hour glass frequently found on Caucasian fabrics, usually in the form of two diamonds joined end to end, signifies the elements of fire and water (Persian blue symbolises air and the zig-zag border water). Whilst the tao-kieh, the purely Chinese symbol of the yin-yang male and female elements, is found in the form of a circle divided into two by a curving line, in each section of which there is a smaller circle.

It should be added that many authorities take the recognition of designs and patterns for granted, even though some of them are extremely complicated and often difficult to differentiate. The beginner should not be discouraged if, at the outset, he fails to be able to 'read' any of the 150-or-so known types of carpet, and if some of the designs do not appear to fit into preconceived notions of who made it and whence it came. Most authorities, it should be remembered, have spent many years working with fabrics and they 'feel' a carpet's origins almost instinctively; it takes a long time to be able to do this but a serious interest should have its own rewards especially if the student looks at, examines and reads about as many carpets as he can.

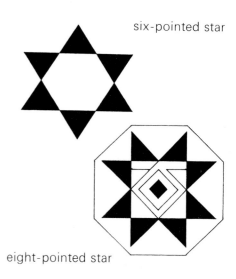

six-pointed star

eight-pointed star

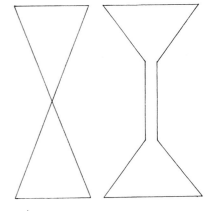

hour glass

yin-yang

3 Persia

Persia has long been renowned as the greatest carpet-weaving country in the world, and it has been estimated that approximately three-quarters of the carpets woven today come from there. The distinguishing characteristic of Persian fabrics is the intricately designed floral pattern woven in glowing colours; only carpets produced in India under the Moghul emperors of the seventeenth century equalled the beauty and majesty of the best Persian products. It is uncertain exactly when weaving began in Persia but it is certainly an extremely long-established art. We read in ancient Persian manuscripts that during the reign of Chosroes I, who was King of Persia from 531 to 579, a carpet called The Spring Carpet

Map of Persia showing centres of carpet production.

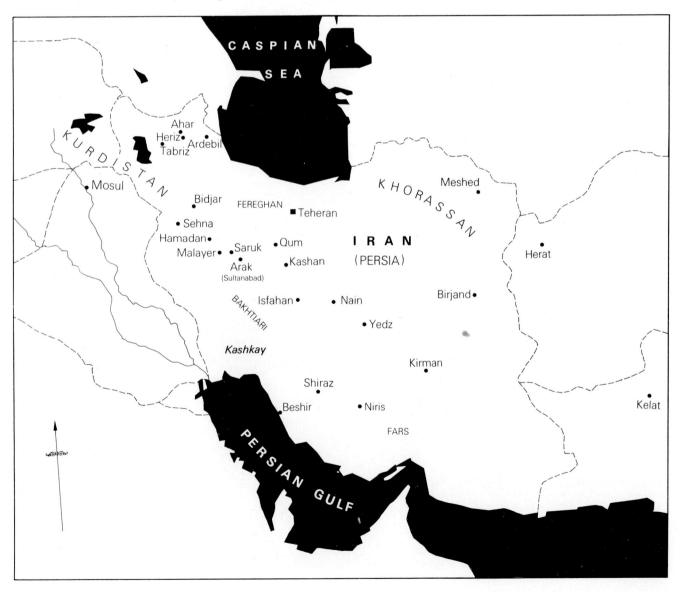

Bidjar carpet (detail).
Persian, 18th century.

Hamadan carpet (detail).
Persian, early 19th century.
The camel-coloured outer border is
often seen on Hamadan pieces.

51

of Chosroes was woven of wool, silk, precious metals, gold and silver and was studded with precious and semi-precious stones. Nothing from this early period survived, though we may assume from the evidence that even then weaving was a well-developed art. Later in time Marco Polo, on his return to Venice in 1295, remarked that the carpets woven at Tabriz were far superior to Indian pieces he had seen.

79 The great period of Persian weaving was the sixteenth century, coming to its zenith under the powerful monarch and patron of the arts Shah Abbas, who ruled from 1586 to 1628, at roughly the same time as another great art-loving emperor, the Moghul ruler Akbar, who will be discussed in the chapter dealing with Indian carpets. It was around this time that most of the very great Persian carpets were woven.

There are approximately sixty-five known types of Persian carpet. The following is a list of the most important ones:

Ardebil	Herat	Lilihan	Sehna
Bakhtiari	Heriz	Meshed	Shiraz
Bakshis	Isfahan	Mosul	Souj-Boulak
Bidjar	Kashan	Nain	Sultanabad
Birjand	Khorassan	Niris	Tabriz
Fereghan	Kirman	Qum	Teheran
Gorevan	Kirmanshah	Saraband	Turkbaff
Hamadan	Kurdistan	Saruk	Yezd

Even with this abbreviated list we still have thirty-two different varieties which the expert must be able to differentiate. The best way to start is to divide the country into four areas as by so doing we will find that carpets in each group generally have characteristics in common.
1 *Western Area:* Ardebil, Bakhtiari, Bakshis, Bidjar, Gorevan, Hamadan, Heriz, Kurdistan, Mosul, Sehna, Souj-Boulak, Tabriz.
2 *Eastern Area:* Birjand, Khorassan, Meshed, Turkbaff.
3 *Central Area:* Fereghan, Isfahan, Kashan, Lilihan, Nain, Qum, Saraband, Saruk, Sultanabad, Teheran, Yezd.
4 *Southern Area:* Kirman, Kirmanshah, Niris, Shiraz.
The odd man out is Herat. Not included here, it will be included later with the Eastern Area carpets. Herat is in fact in Afghanistan although at one time it was part of the Persian Empire, being the capital of Khorassan. Although the carpets associated with Herat are un-questionably Persian, it is thought that they were not in fact woven in the city but were called by the generic name Herat when sold to the West in the early part of this century. This will be discussed in detail later. It should

also be added that Bokhara carpets, associated with Turkestan, were also, and still are, woven in northern Persia. But this again will be discussed later.

We will now examine each of our thirty-two different species and hopefully arrive at certain common denominators for each of our four areas.

1 Carpets from the Western Area of Persia
Ardebil

This is a new name and has only been appearing in conjunction with carpets for about the last twenty years. The type of carpet called by this name has absolutely no connection with the famous sixteenth-century Ardebil carpets discussed above. Modern Ardebil carpets are in fact very Caucasian in character (the town itself is only a few miles south of the border of the Soviet State of Azerbaijan), with geometric borders and large fields covered with geometric shapes, often octagons. The Turkish knot is used and the warp and weft are of cotton.

Bakhtiari

These have been available since the early part of this century and are woven by Kurdish tribesmen who, although originally from the region of Hamadan, have now settled in many villages not far from Isfahan. The designs are that mixture of floral geometricity associated with Hamadan fabrics, frequently using a tile pattern and often a pear-design field. The colour yellow is predominant. Most of the older pieces use the Turkish knot but in more recent examples the Persian knot appears to predominate.

Bakshis

Bakshis is a town in the Heriz district and a number of differently designed carpets appear to have been made there. The antique pieces have fixed all-over floral patterns, usually the herati and the Shah Abbas designs. In the twentieth century, Bakshis motifs changed completely to imitate the geometric, medallion-centred pieces made at Heriz and the neighbouring town of Gorevan. Today it is extremely difficult to decide on stylistic evidence alone what was made where. The Persian knot is usually employed and the warp and the weft are of cotton.

Bidjar

These are woven by Kurdish tribesmen around the town of Bidjar, tribesmen who are thought at one time to have moved west from Saruk. The Turkish knot is used. Whilst the warp and weft of antique examples were usually of

50

Heriz carpet (detail).
Persian, 19th century.

Kurdistan corridor carpet (detail).
Persian, probably woven at
Karaja, mid 18th century.
23 ft × 7 ft 6 in.

wool, the weft was frequently of camel's hair which was often used in an undyed state in the fields of these pieces. Modern examples made in the last twenty years usually have a cotton warp and weft and the Persian knot is now frequently used. Antique and semi-antique Bidjars are considered to be amongst the finest of all Kurdish tribal fabrics; a thick wool was used and although rather coarsely woven, the best carpets were very durable. The herati design was particularly favoured and the field was usually red and woven with a central floral medallion. The modern pieces are generally very heavy and, although keeping to traditional designs, tend to have very garish colours.

Gorevan

Gorevan is a town in the Heriz district. Antique and semi-antique pieces occasionally have the Persian knot but the Turkish is now almost always used. The warp and weft are always of cotton and the carpets are generally very coarsely woven. They are, however, extremely hard-wearing. The predominant colours are blue in the borders with a red field whilst the designs closely follow those of Heriz; there is usually a large geometric medallion centre. Although these carpets are marketed in Tabriz they are generally sold in the West as Heriz, since they are so close in design. Dealers use the word Gorevan as a generic term for all lower-grade Heriz carpets.

Hamadan

51 Although Hamadan carpets are named after the city, many different types, which can be separately identified by experts, are woven in small villages in the vicinity, which is one of the most important and largest carpet-producing areas of Persia. Types such as the Bibikabad, Ingelas, Borchelus, Dergezin, Kabutarhang and Husiana-bad are just some of the many which tend to be known generally as Hamadans. The Turkish knot is usual but the Persian is not infrequently found. The carpets are mostly woven of goat's or camel's hair mixed with wool and cotton. They usually have hexagonal or diamond-shaped designs, especially pole medallions with a field of floral patterns, and few colours are used. The best carpets, however, especially the Bibikabad, Ingelas and Borchelus, are more colourful and are known as Sehna-Hamadans or Sehna-Kurds.

Heriz

54 Like Hamadan, Heriz is a western Persian city which not only produces carpets itself but also lends its name to the

many different types of carpet which are woven in the region. Four of these, Bakshis, Gorevan, Serapi and Tabriz are important enough to be discussed individually, whilst others include Ahar, Bilverdi, Kurdkendi, Mishkin, Jamalabad and Mihriban. Heriz pieces are finer versions of the Gorevan (see above) whilst the best carpets of this type, those woven at Ahar, have only been made since 1958. There are also extremely fine silk carpets from Heriz. In certain old books the name Serapi, after the town of Serab, was given to Heriz and Gorevan pieces of fine quality. Most modern authorities agree that there is no factual evidence for assuming that these carpets were made in Serab; they are more likely to be the best pieces produced in the other two towns mentioned here. Stylistically, they are indistinguishable.

Kurdistan

34, 55

82

This is a slightly misleading description. Strictly speaking, every type of carpet made by nomadic Kurdish tribesmen should be so described, but so many are marketed under the name either of their particular place of manufacture or of the particular Kurdish tribe which made them that Kurdistan now has a more specific meaning and refers to those pieces woven west of Hamadan on the Turkish border. The Turkish knot is used, and the carpets have geometric designs.

Mosul

The town of Mosul is in fact in Iraq and apparently has no connection with the carpets of this name. These are made by nomadic tribesmen on the Turkish border and in the vicinity of Hamadan where they are marketed. They are rather poor quality versions of Hamadan carpets.

Sehna

The city of this name is about a hundred miles north-west of Hamadan and is in fact populated by Kurds, although the characteristics of the famous carpets made there are unlike most fabrics produced by Kurdish tribes. It has given its name to the Sehna or Persian knot which is always used. The finest pieces have a silk warp and weft although cotton is more normally used. Almost all Sehna carpets have an all-over pattern, usually intricately woven, such as the herati and the pear designs; a few examples will have central pole medallions or diamonds. A really fine Sehna carpet is amongst the most densely woven of all Persian fabrics having anything up to a thousand knots to the square inch; needless to say, an antique example in good condition is extremely valuable.

cypress

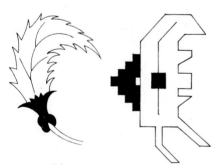

serrated leaves

58

Herat rug.
Persian, early 17th century.

Detail of a large carpet
probably woven at Herat.
Persian, 16th century.
25 ft 10 in × 10 ft 3 in.

Souj-Boulak

This is a Kurdish town north of Tabriz and a few miles east of the Turkish border. As far as is known, no carpets are exported from this town today and the pieces available on the Western market are all more than thirty years old. The Turkish knot is used and whilst the warp and weft are usually of wool, an equal mixture of wool and cotton is fairly common. There is usually an all-over herati pattern on a blue, or occasionally red, field although the Shah Abbas design is also employed. These carpets are generally of a very high standard.

Tabriz

46 Tabriz, the second largest city in Persia, has long been renowned as one of the leading carpet-weaving centres of the world. The Turkish knot is used today although the Persian knot is extensively used in antique pieces. The warp and weft are of cotton with the exception of a few outstanding pieces which use silk. Tabriz is also famous for its silk prayer rugs and for its copies, finely executed in the nineteenth century under European influence, of famous old hunting carpets. Secular pieces will usually have a medallion centre and a tree-of-life design is common. Antique Tabriz carpets are much sought after by collectors.

2 Carpets from the Eastern Area of Persia
Birjand

These are made in the city of Birjand, three hundred miles south of Meshed. Antique carpets were also woven at the village of Daraksh, a few miles to the north-east of Birjand. They have traditionally been woven with the false Persian knot (utilising four rather than two warp threads), thus producing a coarse and loosely woven carpet. They are not considered of good quality even though they are often attractively designed.

herati

Herat

2–3 Herat is the name of a city now situated in Afghanistan
26, 58, 59 but which was until the eighteenth century part of the Khorassan district of Persia. The design invariably used, a small rosette within two lancet-shaped leaves, is known as the herati design. This much is certain, together with the fact that the Turkish knot was used.

There is some doubt as to whether the antique carpets were ever woven in Herat itself. The great authority, A. Cecil Edwards, in his book *The Persian Carpet* published in 1953, suggests convincingly: '... because the Persians used the name Herat in referring to some of these

border herati

carpets, they did not necessarily mean that the carpets were woven in Herat city; . . . the wealthy inhabitants of Herat . . . must have needed carpets for their homes. So the merchants of the city ordered them from the weaving districts of Qainat. When, in time, some of these carpets were sold . . . and found their way to the West, they were called Herat carpets, because they had come from Herat; and not because they had been woven there.'

Another part of the controversy concerns whether any weaving ever has taken place at any time in Herat itself. Edwards states: 'As far as man can remember, no carpets have been woven there; nor does any tradition of weaving exist there. And I know of no locality in Persia where carpets were once produced and which today is producing none.' On the other hand other authorities state that Herat was the seat of a great carpet-weaving industry, and that carpets are still being woven in Herat today. There certainly seem to be two distinct and diametrically opposed schools of thought concerning antique Herat carpets, and two totally contradictory sets of 'facts' about the present-day situation.

Khorassan

This is used as a general term for the two types of carpet woven in this area, Mesheds and Birjands (although Turkbaffs are also woven here they are considered separately). Indeed Khorassan is the name of a province rather than a city. Although we discuss each of these types separately it is worth remembering that a Khorassan can be either one of them; the exact names of the carpets are used mainly to denote quality.

Meshed

Meshed is the capital city of the Khorassan province and one of the Holy Cities of Islam. The tomb of the greatest of the Shea sect saints, Imam Reza, is to be found in the Mosque. Meshed carpets are not actually made in the city itself but in the surrounding villages and, like the Birjands, use a four warp Persian knot although they are of a slightly higher quality. The all-over pear design is the most-used pattern, though a central medallion is often used.

Turkbaff

These carpets, actually made in the city of Meshed, are the only ones from this region of great quality. Turkbaff means Turkish knot, which is employed in the carpets, the looms having been set up at the beginning of this century by weavers from Tabriz. Until the recent im-

Fereghan carpet.
Persian, early 19th century.
The borders contain the characteristic Fereghan
shade of apple green.

portation of synthetic dyes from Switzerland, these were some of the few remaining vegetable-dyed carpets. The all-over pear design is used on the majority of pieces and the field, as on Khorassan carpets, is a purplish red.

3 Carpets from the Central Area of Persia
Fereghan

62 These carpets are made on the plains of Fereghan, to the west of Teheran. The finest antique examples are amongst the most sought-after of all Persian carpets and are very rare; traditionally the Persian knot has been used although more recently the Turkish knot has been employed. The warp and weft are nearly always of cotton. There are basically two types of Fereghan: the all-over pattern and the medallion centre. The former usually has the herati design which, because it is so often found on these carpets, is sometimes known as the Fereghan pattern. The medallion-centred pieces are rarer and more valuable. One distinguishing characteristic of these carpets is their frequent use of an unusual shade of apple green especially in the borders.

Isfahan

63 Isfahan, the old capital of Persia, is one of the greatest weaving cities of the world and the carpets produced there during the sixteenth and seventeenth centuries are probably the most magnificent ever made. The city itself with its two great Mosques, the Shah and the Lutfulla, is a worthy setting. The Persian knot was and is used whilst the warp and weft have always been of cotton and occasionally silk on the finest pieces.

Probably the greatest existing carpet from Isfahan (or possibly Kashan) is the Austrian royal hunting carpet
19 in Vienna, although some authorities claim that, Maqsud
18 or no, the Ardebil Mosque carpet was woven there also. Apart from this type, two other kinds, the animal carpets, similar to hunting carpets but without human figures on
38 horseback, and vase carpets, so-called because a motif resembling a vase of flowers is repeated in the field, are representative of the famous antique pieces which may or may not have been woven at Isfahan.

If they were not woven there, the two most popular alternatives would seem to be either Tabriz or Herat. There are approximately 1,500 carpets surviving from the sixteenth and seventeenth centuries.

Between approximately 1722, when the city was overrun by Afghan tribesmen, to the beginning of this century, no carpets were produced at Isfahan, or at least no carpets were exported. The carpets produced early on in

vase of flowers

this century were not of particularly good quality, but in recent years the standard has improved considerably and modern Isfahan pieces, using traditional designs, are much in demand.

66 A type of carpet associated with Isfahan, and which indeed is often called by that name, is made in the village of Joshagan a few miles west of Kashan. This type was made during the seventeenth and eighteenth centuries and is still made today. The main design used has remained the same and consists of small floral shapes in diamond patterns over the field, in the centre of which is usually a diamond medallion, whilst each corner of the field has a triangular medallion. The fields of the older pieces are invariably ivory or blue whilst the modern ones, which are very fine, are red. Another type of carpet thought to have been woven here is the so-called tree carpet in which the wide field is covered with a variety of trees and ferns.

Kashan

67 Kashan, about 150 miles south of Teheran, is another of the great carpet-weaving cities of Persia and it was here
18 that the Ardebil carpets were almost certainly made. As with Isfahan, no carpets were woven here during the eighteenth and nineteenth centuries for export, and indeed the best carpets woven there today are not exported, much to the chagrin of European and American dealers. The floral carpets made at the beginning of this century are generally very large and of very fine quality. The field is covered with swirling flowers with a central, diamond-shaped medallion. Kashan is also famous for its silk prayer rugs which are often woven with columns on each side of the mihrab and bouquets of flowers or the tree of life, and the mosque lamp hanging within the niche itself. The Persian knot is used and the warp and weft are of either cotton or silk. It is also worth noting that a few carpets woven at the beginning of this century use superb merino wool.

Lilihan

Although made in the town of Lilihan mid-way between Sultanabad and Isfahan, the carpets are in fact woven by Persian Armenians who probably entered the country in flight from the Turks during the First World War and settled in and around Lilihan. The carpets are Turkish-Caucasian in character, usually have a floral field in a geometric style and are generally bleached and painted. They began to appear in the West in the mid 1920s but apparently ceased to be woven around the beginning of

Joshagan carpet.
Persian, early 19th century.

Medallion carpet probably
woven at Kashan.
Persian, late 17th century.

the Second World War. They are not generally of very good quality although they can be attractive.

lily and iris

Nain

70
The town of Nain lies half-way between Teheran and Kirman in central Persia and about eighty miles east of Isfahan, of which city it is considered a suburb. Most authorities agree that the finest carpets being woven in Persia at the present time come from here. The design most frequently used is the Shah Abbas on a cream ground with a central circular medallion and triangular corners. The main border is usually on a blue ground. These carpets are of modern production.

Qum

Qum is the name of a town ninety miles south of Teheran and approximately 180 miles from Nain. The carpets made here are very similar in design to Nain pieces and like them have only been in production for a few years. The quality is almost equal and it requires an experienced and expert eye to tell them apart.

Saraband (and Mir-Saraband)

These are named after the district of Sarawan not far from Sultanabad. The antique carpets from this district were woven in the town of Mirabad and are known as Mirs or Mir-Sarabands. The antique piece is very distinctive for several reasons. Firstly, the weft thread is always dyed blue. Secondly, the borders almost always have a vine or Mir pattern on an ivory ground. Thirdly, the field is almost always red or deep blue; and finally, the field is invariably covered with rows of pear designs in either blue or red depending on the field colour. Indeed there is a tendency for any carpet which bears a superficial resemblance to a Mir to be called a Saraband. The only variations on the pear design are an all-over herati design or the herati design with the medallion centre.

The modern Saraband follows the Mir design, although it always uses the pear pattern and always (at least for the past fifty years) has a red field. It is not, as is usual with modern pieces, so finely woven. It should be remembered that certain Saruk carpets are today woven to the Saraband pattern and are possibly superior. An expert can tell them apart by the finer weave of the Saruk. The warp and weft of both old and new pieces are of cotton, and the Persian knot is used. A further distinguishing characteristic of Mirs is their odd weave, which admittedly can only be deciphered by an expert, where every alternate knot is doubled under the other.

Saruk

The real antique Saruks were woven in the town of that name twenty miles north-west of Sultanabad. However, the majority of the thousands of rugs woven this century which are called Saruks were certainly not woven there but in Sultanabad itself; they bear only a superficial resemblance to the earlier carpets. The antique has a cotton warp and weft, usually has a medallion centre and is very finely woven.

The majority of the twentieth-century so-called Saruks have an all-over detached floral design on a rose ground and can be very attractive. They were particularly popular in America and vast quantities were imported to that country before the Second World War. Unfortunately, a high percentage of these were chemically washed and then painted in order to give them a mellow look, a process which has had over the years a serious effect on the condition of the carpet.

It should be noted that to the west of Sultanabad lies the Malayer area in which two important carpet-weaving towns, Josan and Malayer itself, are situated. These types both have the Turkish knot, unlike the Saruk which has the Persian, but their designs are based very closely on antique Saruks. Josan carpets are considered amongst the finest being produced in Persia today. Most of them, like old Saruks, are in rug sizes.

Sultanabad

The town of Sultanabad is the centre of one of the largest carpet-weaving areas of Persia. Within its boundaries, the following towns are situated: Malayer, Muskabad, Qum, Kashan, Mahal, Lilihan, Khussar and Saruk. The plains of Fereghan are also part of this area. We have discussed Fereghan, Kashan, Lilihan, Qum and Saruk pieces separately. Here we will examine Sultanabad carpets proper and Mahals. We shall also discuss the fact that in the trade today Muskabad, Mahal and Arak are words denoting the quality of carpets made here.

The principal carpet woven in this area is the Saruk, discussed in detail above. In general all other carpets made in the vicinity are copies of, or variations on, this design. The main variation is called Sultanabad, was made in that city and was at one time a distinctive type. The carpets usually referred to by this name were made about twenty or more years ago and have floral, especially the Shah Abbas, designs. In recent times, the carpets produced in Sultanabad and in the surrounding villages and towns have become more dependent on the Saruk designs, although there is a wide variation of quality.

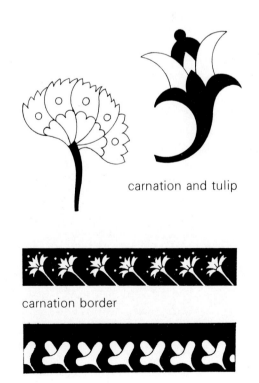

carnation and tulip

carnation border

69

Nain carpet.
Persian, first half 20th century.
The cream ground with blue borders is typical.

Teheran carpet.
Persian, early 20th century.
This and the previous piece show Western influence in the colours and designs.

Quasi-Saruk carpets are therefore graded into three qualities which are Arak, called after the modern Persian name for the city of Sultanabad, Mahal, meaning village-made, and Muskabad, the poorest of all the carpets made in this vicinity. It takes an expert to tell the difference between the various types of Saruk-Sultanabad pieces and the average student should not bother himself too much with something about which even the authorities are none too sure.

Teheran

71 Teheran is the capital of Persia and has given its name to the carpets which are woven in the suburbs of the city; it is probable that the finest of these, equal in quality to the Isfahans, are not exported. Teheran carpets have been produced only since the beginning of this century; the warp and weft are of cotton and the Persian knot is used. The herati design is frequently employed whilst prayer rugs woven with the tree of life are not unusual.

Yezd

Although made in central Persia, Yezd pieces are described by different authorities as being allied either to those made at Tabriz or to those at Kirman, even though Tabriz is just over seven hundred miles from Yezd, Yezd is two hundred miles from Kirman and Tabriz is nearly a thousand miles from Kirman. There is, however, no doubt that antique examples can often be mistaken for Tabriz carpets with their use of the herati design on a blue field. Warp and weft are of cotton and the knot is Turkish, the same as that used at Tabriz. It is interesting to note that Yezd was a renowned silk-producing city whilst Tabriz was famous for its silk carpets.

tree of life

The modern Yezd pieces, however, are different. The influence is now solely Kirman, a style which was probably copied for economic reasons early this century when Kirman carpets were one of the most popular of all Persian carpets on the Western market. Yezd carpets now usually have a red field with a floral medallion and matching floral corners. They also now employ the Persian knot which is used in Kirman pieces.

4 Carpets from the Southern Area of Persia
Kirman

74 The city of Kirman is the centre of a large and important weaving area. Several villages and small towns, apart from the city itself, are engaged in this industry, the most important of which are Ravar, Okalat-Dehzanuw, Anaristan, Mahan, Saidabad, Anar, Zarand, Khanuk and

Chatrud. An interesting historical note is that Paisley shawls, employing the pear design found on so many Persian carpets, were woven in Kirman amongst other places for the European market during the nineteenth century.

Kirman is an ancient city (Marco Polo commented favourably upon it) and carpets have probably been woven in the area for centuries; it was only during the second half of the nineteenth century, however, that any were exported and those were new. Indeed, the oldest Kirman carpets have generally been made within the last hundred years.

The earliest Kirmans were woven with the most naturalistic designs of any Oriental carpets. They usually have an ivory field and depict well-drawn animals, birds, human figures and flowers. A frequently used design was an all-over pattern of baskets of roses, again very realistically delineated. The colours on old Kirmans are usually soft pastel shades; the Persian knot is always used and the warp and weft are of cotton. A very small number of silk pieces were woven and these are now of course extremely valuable.

Modern Kirmans are very different. The colours still tend to be pastel shades with a predominant use of the ivory ground but the carpets made in the 1920s and 1930s up to the present conformed to the prevailing American demand for floral carpets similar in design to French eighteenth- and nineteenth-century examples. This taste the Kirmans successfully satisfied with floral borders and medallion centres. Since the Second World War a third type, utilising the bright reds and blues so much admired by the Persians themselves, has been woven specifically for the domestic market.

Kirmanshah

This is a name which has caused and still causes considerable confusion and is only included here for curiosity's sake. Kirmanshah is a Kurdish town in northwest Persia, about 650 miles from Kirman and 280 miles south of Tabriz. Many books simply point out the distances and blindly state that for all that Kirmanshahs look very like Kirmans. The indications are, however, that Kirmanshah carpets as we know them have no connection with the remote Kurdish town of the same name. It may be that 'Kirmanshah' was originally a word meant to denote a superior kind of Kirman, although, according to Lewis in *The Practical Book of Oriental Rugs*, Kirmanshah was a great caravan centre whence these carpets were shipped west. They have the Persian

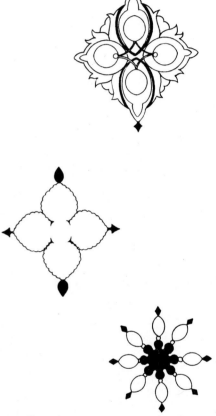

medallions

73

Shiraz 'mille-fleurs' prayer rug.
Persian, 18th century.

Large hunting carpet possibly woven at Kirman (detail).
Persian, 17th or 18th century.
26 ft 8 in × 10 ft 9 in.

knot and a cotton warp and weft, none of these being Kurdish characteristics, and the designs are usually intricately floral.

Niris

These carpets are made by the hill tribes in the province of Laristan. Niris is the name of a salt lake in the area, which is dominated by the great carpet-weaving city of Shiraz. The Persian knot is generally employed although on older pieces the Turkish knot was sometimes used; the warp and weft are of wool. Niris carpets are on the whole more tightly woven than Shiraz pieces and they are distinctively designed and coloured. The pear design, woven in rows and usually in green, is found on a madder-red field. There are approximately five border stripes which mainly employ the barber-pole design. The wool is almost always of very good quality and these carpets are greatly respected by collectors.

Shiraz

75 The city of Shiraz is the centre of the great south-Persian carpet-weaving area, which includes pieces woven by the Kashkai and Khamseh tribes and those woven around Beshir and Lake Niris. Amongst the individual names given to Shiraz-area carpets, apart from Shiraz itself, are Niris, Faristan, Kashkai, Nifliz and Afshar. Shiraz is the capital of the province of Faristan or Fars and is the market place for all the carpets woven in the region, with the exception of the Afshars which are marketed at the city of Kirman.

Antique Shiraz carpets used better wool than just about all other Persian carpets, and those woven today still employ wool for the warp and the weft. The pear pattern was frequently used, as well as pole medallions and diamond medallions into which were woven stylised birds and animals (the bird is said to have represented the nightingale, a symbol of peace). The Persian knot is generally used but the Turkish knot is occasionally found, an interesting complement to the slightly northern geometricity of some Shiraz designs. Old books often refer to the prayer rugs from here as Mecca Shiraz since they were apparently favoured by pilgrims to the Holy City.

We have now come to the conclusion of our individual examinations of the thirty-two main kinds of Persian carpet. Before making some general points about these different types, we must mention a variety of Persian carpet which does not fit into any category.

Polonaise

78, 79 In the Paris Exhibition of 1878, Prince Czartoryski, a Polish nobleman from Warsaw, showed some floral carpets superbly woven with silk and gold and silver threads. They did not appear to resemble any known type of carpet, although they were clearly of Persian inspiration. They were therefore called Polonaise, the French word for Polish. It is now known that several silk carpets were presented by the Persian Shahs to various European rulers, and it is interesting to note that the majority of the 350 or so surviving examples of these carpets are now in European museums. Obviously a gift from one monarch to another would have to be something of great value, a fact which explains the magnificent quality of these pieces. Modern scholars generally accept that they were woven on the royal looms in Persia, probably at Isfahan, and that they were all made in the sixteenth and early seventeenth centuries. There is no evidence to support the theory that they were woven in Poland by Persian weavers sent there by request of the king and this idea is now disregarded by all authorities.

Conclusion

The geographical locations into which we divided Persia at the beginning of this section also denote strong stylistic differences in the various types of carpets produced.

The Kurdish nomad tribes dominate the western area, intermingled with Armenians from the Caucasus. Nomadic tribes from Turkey have also been wandering back and forth across the Turko-Persian border for centuries. In old books, the north-west area of Persia was usually referred to as Kurdistan and this name, as we have said before, was often, and still is sometimes, taken 34, 55, 82 to refer to all the carpets made in this particular area.

The most obvious characteristics of Persian carpets, the Persian knot and ornate floral designs, are generally lacking in the fabrics produced in this part of the country; these generally employ the Turkish knot and the designs have a bold geometricity which we shall see to be the main feature of both Turkish and Caucasian fabrics. As with the other three sections of the country, there is in western Persia a city which itself is the centre and focal point of the carpet-weaving industry, namely Heriz, and which has taken the place of Kurdistan in describing the general type of carpet woven here.

However, one of those annoying inconsistencies which generalities tend to produce is that within this predominantly Kurdish area with its non-Persian type of carpet is the Kurdish city of Sehna which not only has given its

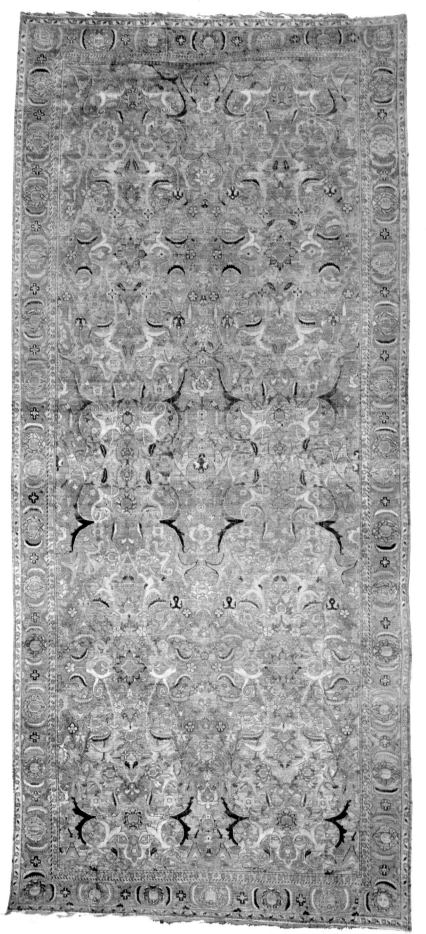

'Polonaise' carpet from Isfahan.
Persian, 17th century.
Woven in silk with gold and
silver threads.

'Polonaise' rug from Isfahan.
Persian, early 17th century.
Woven on the court looms
during the reign of Shah Abbas.

name to the Persian knot but has also produced carpets which, stylistically, are not Kurdish but pure Persian.

The eastern part of the country is dominated by, ironically, the Afghan town of Herat, although this was, as we have said, once part of Persia. This is not a large carpet-weaving area and the main design of an all-over pear pattern is the most common distinguishing feature, although these are not the only types of Persian carpet which use this design.

Central Persia, the largest and the most prolific of our four areas, is dominated by the two centres of Kashan and Sultanabad which are also, as is Heriz in western Persia, the main market places. In general the carpets woven here tend to be the most characteristic of all Persian fabrics; when one thinks of the words 'Persian carpet' the picture that springs to the mind's eye – a large carpet richly woven with vari-coloured flowers often with a central medallion – is almost certain to closely resemble an Isfahan or Kashan piece. The Persian knot is generally used and this area has produced most of the great master-pieces of Persian weaving.

Carpets woven in the south have as their market places the two great cities of Kirman and Shiraz. As with eastern carpets, the most popular southern design tends to be the all-over pear pattern but southern carpets are much finer creations and more valuable. The design of those carpets woven under the aegis of Kirman are generally more floral than those made near Shiraz, which have a certain geometric quality; the Kirman area, it should be noted, is by far the larger of the two.

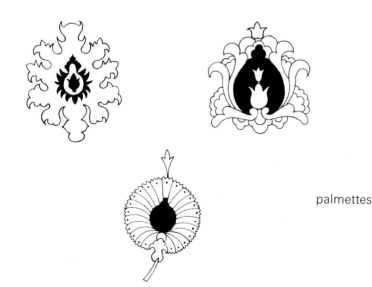

palmettes

4 Turkey

Carpet-weaving has probably been taking place in Turkey for at least as long as it has been in Persia; indeed, apart from the Russian Pazyryk carpet, the earliest carpet we know of, the Dragon and the Phoenix carpet in Berlin, may have been woven in Turkey. The exceptional beauty of this piece clearly has for the present-day student the same implication as does the Russian piece, namely that for it to have been produced at all carpet-weaving must have already had a long and skilful tradition behind it.

During the sixteenth and seventeenth centuries, carpets obviously made in Turkey appear continually in paintings by famous artists. Indeed, so often were they used by Holbein, as in his famous painting of *The Ambassadors* in the National Gallery, London, that these pieces, probably woven at Oushak, came to be called Holbein carpets. Turkish carpets also appear in fifteenth-century Flemish paintings, including several by Jan van Eyck, and they are depicted in many Italian paintings, and, significantly, most often in portraits executed by Venetians. Venice was the richest trading port in Europe and

Map of Turkey showing centres of carpet production.

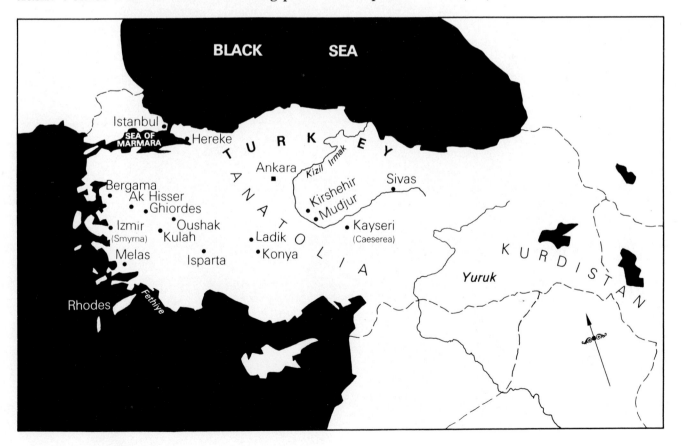

Large Kurdistan carpet woven to a Herat design (detail).
Persian, early 19th century.
26 ft × 10 ft 8 in.

'Holbein' carpet.
Turkish, *c.* 1600.
Metropolitan Museum of Art, New York.
Gift of Joseph V. McMullan 1961.

the large number of Turkish carpets which we can assume were in the homes of the rich Venetian merchant class no doubt were part of their trade with the East.

It is known, for instance, that Cardinal Wolsey, Lord Chancellor of England, purchased sixty Turkish carpets from a Venetian merchant to furnish his palace at Hampton Court, carpets which His Eminence referred to as Damascene since the rich designs resembled Damascene work, the Eastern art of inlaying gold, silver and copper into brass. At the time the Holbein portraits were painted, in the first half of the sixteenth century, Turkey had become the strongest country in the Middle East, brought to greatness by its legendary ruler Suliman the Magnificent, called The Grand Turk.

Turkish carpets have certain distinguishing features. Firstly they always employ the Turkish knot; secondly the warp and weft of all carpets made before about 1870 are either of wool or goat's hair. Since that time, cotton has been used. This is a point worth watching if one is under the impression that one is buying a Turkish carpet which is a hundred years old or more. Thirdly, all Turkish carpets have wool or cotton double, flat-woven side cords; only two Persian types, the Tabriz and the Heriz, have this feature. Old Turkish carpets rarely have living creatures, either animal or human, woven into them, as a result of religious pressures against figural images; in the present century, however, such strictures have been relaxed, or ignored; moreover, the sacred colour green is now used fairly regularly in most types of carpets. Finally, large Turkish carpets tend to have been made in the last sixty or seventy years.

There are approximately thirty different varieties of Turkish carpet; the following is a list of the eighteen most important ones which, as we have done with our selected Persian types, we shall examine individually:

Ak Hisser Dimirdji Kirshehir Ladik Mudjur Smyrna
Anatolia   Ghiordes Konya   Makri Oushak Sparta
Bergama   Hereke   Kulah   Melas Sivas   Yuruk

Most of the other types of Turkish carpet are versions of the above which only the scholar can differentiate. Indeed many of those mentioned here are fairly difficult to recognise. However, as they are all names likely to be met with fairly often, they are worth looking at separately. Before we do so, it should be said that during the seventeenth century beautiful and very Persian-looking floral carpets were woven in Turkey, probably on the royal looms at Istanbul.

Ak Hisser

These carpets are named after the town about sixty miles north-east of Izmir. They have large medallions and geometric designs similar to those which appear on Oushak and Ghiordes pieces. However, no carpets which can definitely be assigned to this town have been made for roughly the last fifty years. Indeed there seems to be a considerable amount of controversy concerning what Ak Hisser carpets really look like. It is a name which is used fairly regularly for carpets that could quite easily be from Oushak, Ghiordes or even Kirshehir.

Anatolia

This is a slightly confusing term which needs a little explanation. Anatolia is a synonym for that part of Turkey which is in Asia, traditionally called Asia Minor. Anatolian carpets, therefore, are Turkish carpets, not a very helpful definition. However, the term is now generally used for carpets obviously from Turkey but to which no specific place or maker's name can be attached. It is also often applied to modern Turkish carpets woven with Persian floral designs.

Bergama

15, 87 Bergama is a small town about sixty miles north of Izmir on the site of ancient Pergamum. The carpets have deep, full-bodied colours and are fairly rare on the market today. They usually have a geometric medallion centre and are similar to Ladik pieces. They also have a certain similarity to Kazak carpets from the Caucasus. In the 1920s, a cheap carpet made in Turkey and Greece was marketed as Pergamo. These were not made in the town of the same name nor were they of any quality.

Dimirdji

The town of Dimirdji is half way between Ghiordes and Oushak. As far as is known, no carpets have been made there for at least fifty years. Dimirdji carpets invariably have a distinctive hexagon centre which has a red ground, the four corners of the field usually woven in green, and the borders predominantly yellow. They are of considerable rarity.

Ghiordes

43, 90 The city of Ghiordes which has given its name to the Turkish knot is about seventy miles east of Izmir. The carpets made there are considered amongst the greatest of all Turkish fabrics. It is poetic justice that the Turkish knot should be called Ghiordes, since this is the ancient

Rare Istanbul rug.
Turkish, early 17th century.
Probably woven on the Ottoman court looms.

Bergama rug.
Turkish, 17th century.

city of Gordium which gave its name to the Gordian knot cut by Alexander the Great.

Ghiordes pieces can be divided into three kinds: antique carpets, prayer rugs and modern carpets. To take the last first, modern Ghiordes pieces bear no resemblance, either in design or quality, to antique examples. They are very poor and use Persian designs. Most recent carpet books show a surprising unanimity in either ignoring them completely or dismissing them.

Our first category should for clarity's sake perhaps be referred to as antique secular carpets and rugs since it is meant to indicate anything which is not a prayer rug. The first point to be made about these is that they are amongst the only Turkish secular carpets which have considerable amounts of green. In many books it is said that green was never used except on prayer rugs but experience shows this to be incorrect. The secular pieces generally have geometric all-over patterns on an ivory or magenta field. When we said above that Ghiordes carpets are thought of as being the greatest Turkish fabrics, we should perhaps have qualified this statement. Ghiordes prayer rugs unquestionably are amongst the finest of their kind made anywhere in the world; the secular pieces, however, do not tend to be so fine although they hardly merit C. W. Jacobsen's stricture that they are at the bottom rung of old Turkish carpets.

Ghiordes prayer rugs are amongst the most sought-after of all Oriental carpets and are distinctive in design. They nearly always have three wide borders of different geometric patterns between which are three very narrow stripes. In the centre of the carpet is the mihrab or niche which has a lamp hanging from the arch in many examples. The two panels at either end of the niche are filled with a geometric design, as are the areas within the centre square on either side of the inverted V-shaped arch. The colours are usually rich and varied. The late seventeenth-century examples, however, tend to be different in design.

Hereke

91 Hereke is a town in north west Turkey on the shores of the Sea of Marmara. A factory was established there by the Sultan of Turkey and subsidised by him. Hereke carpets are almost totally un-Turkish in character for the simple reason that the weavers were all imported from Kirman in Persia. Their only concession to Turkey is that they employ the Turkish knot. Their designs closely follow those of Kirman carpets with naturalistic all-over floral patterns such as the Shah Abbas design whilst animals, rare creatures in normal Turkish fabrics,

Ghiordes scorpion

are frequently found. They also follow the antique Kirmans in using soft pastel colours. Silk Herekes are probably the finest ever woven and often employ silver and gold thread. The high standard of old Hereke carpets, which are extremely valuable, demonstrates more clearly than anything that they were woven on royal looms.

Kirshehir
These carpets are made in the town of this name a hundred miles south-east of Ankara. They are always in the form of prayer rugs and use a large quantity of a distinctive bright grass green. They also always have the three-headed flower motif in the borders. They are noted for their strong but perfectly balanced use of colour.

Konya
Konya, often spelt Konieh, is the ancient city of Iconium and is approximately 150 miles south of Ankara. The carpets generally use bland mellow colours such as browns and creams which have a beautifully harmonious effect. They normally come in the form of prayer rugs which have a selection of unrelated abstract designs within the mihrab. Secular pieces often have a double pole medallion made up of two octagons. Their designs are, on the whole, crude and they are not well woven.

Kulah
94 Being only fifty miles from Ghiordes, carpets woven at Kulah are extremely similar to those made in the neighbouring town. Like Ghiordes pieces, Kulahs are generally prayer rugs which, if they are antiques, are amongst the most admired of all Turkish carpets. The main difference between a Ghiordes and a Kulah prayer rug is that the latter usually has only one crossbar which is located above the niche. And the niche itself does not reach the crossbar as it does in a Ghiordes but only goes about two-thirds of the way up the field. An interesting design peculiar to the Kulah is the prayer rug with a double-ended mihrab; this is known as a Kourmur Jur Kulah. The design is woven so as not to give an approximate architectural representation but is merely outlined in white on a geometrically patterned field. Kulah prayer rugs are also often found with one or two rows of cypress trees on a boat-shaped ground symbolising the soul sailing into the world to come. These rugs are known as tomb rugs.

Ladik
42, 95 Ladik is a small town near Konya, and in ancient times was called Laodicea. Ladik carpets are extremely rare

Ghiordes prayer rug.
Turkish, late 18th century.
This design is usually found on
late 17th-century pieces.

Hereke carpet.
Turkish, early 19th century.
Silk pile with metal threads,
characteristic pastel colours.

and very few have been woven since about 1930. Those of the nineteenth century and earlier are amongst the most beautiful and valuable of all Oriental carpets. The majority of pieces made here are prayer rugs although there are a number of small mats about two feet by three feet. The colours used are predominantly rich reds, pale greens and blues. The prayer niche frequently has a characteristic shape with a stepped arch, each step having a latch-hook pattern in the large panel always to be found above the arch. Some antique examples have a characteristic triple arch in the mihrab and a panel of tulips upside-down at the base.

Makri

Makri carpets were probably woven in the islands and coastal towns of the gulf of Makri, now called Fethiye, in southern Turkey. The largest island in this vicinity is Rhodes which, at its most northerly point, is only about twenty-five miles from the Turkish coast; Makri carpets are often known as Rhodian, which has led some authorities to believe that at one time they were woven solely on this island. They come mainly in the form of prayer rugs and are brightly coloured, usually with a rich blue field on which are woven large, bold, geometric designs in a predominant shade of apricot yellow. One recognisable characteristic is the frequent use of two mihrabs side by side with both ends arched, separated by a thin column. Occasionally the rugs are woven with three mihrabs and sometimes with one but the most usual bright, all-over design, which gives an impression of zig-zags covering the whole surface, is easy to recognise and remember.

Melas

These were woven in small towns and villages south of Izmir and marketed in the town of Melas, thus the name Melas is used to describe all of those carpets woven in the area. Weaving has been practically non-existent there during the present century so almost all Melas carpets are antiques. For this reason, and also because they are extremely fine, examples in good condition are rare and valuable. Most pieces are prayer rugs which have their own distinctive mihrab shape, resembling a diamond surmounting a quadrilateral. The field of the mihrab is usually of a rich red-brown and the designs are most frequently woven in an ivory colour.

Mudjur

Mudjur carpets are named after the town of Mudjur in central Turkey not far from Kirshehir. No carpets of any

Mudjur stepped mihrab

95

92

quality have been made since the First World War. They are almost all antiques, therefore, and although not quite so highly thought of as, for instance, pieces from Ghiordes and Ladik, they are extremely valuable if in fine condition, probably on the same level as the Melas. Like most of the greatest Turkish weaving, Mudjurs are nearly always prayer rugs and have a distinctive stepped mihrab surmounted by a small tower. The field of the mihrab is almost always a deep rich red.

Oushak

47, 98 During the sixteenth and seventeenth centuries, the city of Oushak, about seventy miles east of Ghiordes, was the greatest weaving city in Turkey, if not the world. Needless to say, almost all the carpets from this period are now in museums and should not be confused with the crudely made and crudely coloured carpets made there this century. Antique Oushaks, examples of which frequently appear in seventeenth-century and earlier paintings, are amongst the most Persian-looking of all Turkish carpets, a fact which has led many scholars to believe that they were woven by immigrant Persian artisans; there seems little evidence to support this theory. The usual colour scheme of an antique Oushak is a large red field with corner medallions and a central medallion in blue and red made up of fluid geometric forms resembling crystalline structures. Both the Metropolitan Museum and the Victoria and Albert Museum have superb early examples in their collections.

Sivas

These carpets are made in and around the city of Sivas in central Turkey. The best examples are almost always seventy years old or more and bear little relation to the inferior examples made in the last twenty years. There seems to be a certain amount of confusion concerning these pieces. Lewis, in his book, states that the designs are distinctly Turkish in character, whilst Jack Franses remarks that they are often mistaken for Persian and illustrates an example which would seem to prove his point. They were indeed amongst the most finely woven of all Turkish carpets and, with their arabesque medallions, somewhat resemble Oushaks.

Smyrna

99 Smyrna, now called Izmir, for centuries one of Turkey's principal sea-ports, is not, nor ever was, a carpet-weaving city, but was a market place for those carpets woven in the neighbouring towns and villages. Thus it is a rather

Kulah prayer rug.
Turkish, early 19th century.

Ladik prayer rug.
Turkish,
late 18th century.
Note the upside-down
tulips at the base of
the mihrab.

misleading name which is only included here since it is so often found in carpet literature as well as in auction and dealers' catalogues. The name is frequently used as a generic term for twentieth-century Oushak and Ghiordes carpets and denotes a modern piece of poor quality. It is also often used in reference to the Persian-looking carpets made at Sivas and Isparta which were treated with caution. The most typical design for a carpet is an elongated hexagonal field edged along the inside with trefoil sprigs of flowers.

Sparta

Sparta is a corruption of Isparta, the town 150 miles west of Konya in and around which these carpets were woven. Sparta carpets were made by Armenians, many of whom fled from Turkey during the First World War settling in Piraeus and Salonika in Greece. Sparta carpets therefore may be either from Turkey or Greece. They are generally of poor quality and imitate Persian rather than Turkish designs; they have pedantic and unattractive floral patterns. Although occasionally an example of good quality is to be found, they are not generally highly regarded.

Yuruk

Yuruk means mountaineer. These carpets are woven by Nomadic Kurdish hill tribes in eastern Turkey, the same people who inhabit north-west Persia and the Caucasus. They are Caucasian in character, using such typical designs as swastikas and latch hooks. The main field is usually woven with three diamond medallions, either conjoined or separate, and the colours are usually rich red-browns, blues and purples. Yuruks also contain more green than most Turkish fabrics, which is usually of a rather cloying shade.

Before moving on to the conclusion, we should perhaps describe one other very special type of Turkish carpet, which is discussed in detail by Jack Franses in his book *European and Oriental Rugs*. This is the Koum ka Pour (meaning gates to the sands) which type was woven for a period of only about twenty years, between roughly 1890 and 1910, in a suburb of Istanbul. They were woven under royal patronage by the master Turkish weaver Kanata and are Persian-floral in character. They are characterised by their use of gold and silver threads which were woven into decorative flower patterns of many colours. Of exceptional beauty and rarity, these carpets, unlike any others ever woven in Turkey, have a place in the history of carpet-weaving which may be compared to that of Fabergé, the late nineteenth-century Russian gold-smith, in the field of applied arts. Koum ka Pours are described by Mr Franses, a dealer of considerable experience, as being amongst the greatest carpets ever made.

Conclusion

Unlike Persia, Turkey does not appear to be particularly active in the carpet-weaving field today. It will have been noted that almost all Turkish carpets woven this century are of poor quality and bear little resemblance to the fine antique pieces whose names they bear. We have also demonstrated two basic points. Firstly, Turkish carpets tend to be geometric in design and use rich colours. The main exception to this is Oushak which is more Persian, i.e. floral, in appearance, although Sivas and Sparta fabrics are also more floral than is normal.

The second point to be noted is that the majority of Turkish carpets come in the form of prayer rugs, and in many cases we have noted above they have distinctive mihrab shapes by which they can be easily recognised. Again, the principal exception to this statement is Oushak which has produced large carpets, some being as much as twenty-five by fifty feet.

Finally, it is perhaps worth noting that as Turkey has never been nearly so prolific a carpet-weaving country as Persia, fine antique examples tend to be a great deal rarer than their Persian counterparts. The finest Ghiordes, Ladik and Oushak pieces are as expensive, if not more so, than any carpets made elsewhere. Because Turkish pieces of great age and quality are so rarely seen on the market, the well-publicised high prices paid for Persian and Indian pieces may well have caused some people to get the impression that they are not so valuable; such an idea would be completely wrong.

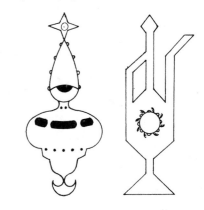

lamp and jug

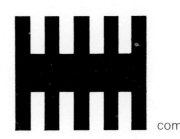

comb

Smyrna rug.
Turkish, late 18th or
early 19th century.

Large Oushak medallion carpet (detail).
Turkish, early 17th century.
22 ft × 12 ft.

5 The Caucasus

Between the Black Sea to the west and the Caspian to the east lie several Soviet States, the most important of which are Georgia, Armenia, Azerbaijan and the Russian Federated Socialist Republic (which includes the State of Daghestan). These States make up the area in which most Caucasian carpets were made. They are populated by many different peoples and tribes and there are two main religions, Christianity and Islam. Until the nineteenth century the Caucasus was part of Persia who ceded it to Imperial Russia. Because of this vast commingling of peoples who also wandered into Turkey and Persia, Caucasian carpets have been a source of confusion, even to experts.

However, if we take some long-established classifications we will be able to differentiate some of the most well-known and characteristic Caucasian carpets.

Of the nineteen or twenty names which have at some time been chosen to describe these pieces, we have selected eleven of the most widely used:

Baku	Derbend	Karabagh	Shirvan
Chi-Chi	Erivan	Kazak	Soumak
Daghestan	Kabistan	Kuba	

Map of Caucasus showing centres of carpet production.

It can be safely stated that a Caucasian carpet by any other name will turn out to be a particular variant of one of the above to which a trade name has been attached. It need only be added that the word Armenian is often used, somewhat misleadingly, in older books as a synonym for Caucasian.

Baku

These carpets are named after the city of Baku, a sea-port on the Caspian now in the Soviet State of Azerbaijan. It is the port where carpets manufactured in the city itself and in the immediate vicinity are marketed. Almost all these are more than fifty years old and can be recognised by their distinctive pattern. This always consists of a field of large rectilinear pear motifs which, in the case of this particular type of carpet, tend to resemble fir-cones more than pears; they are arranged in rows on a field on which several octagonal medallions may also appear. The field colour is invariably dark blue, whilst the pears are usually woven in shades of cream, ivory and yellow.

Chi-Chi

These are made by a tribe called the Tchechen, by which name they are often known, which inhabits the mountains of north-west Daghestan. Chi-Chi carpets are nearly always more than fifty years old, are rare, and extremely popular with collectors. They have their own distinctive design. The field, always either dark blue or dark red, is woven with a minute, all-over mosaic pattern, on which there are rows of small octagons, again made up of mosaics. One of the borders at least always has rows of eight-petalled flowers, which are often woven between the bars of a Greek meander.

Chi-Chi star border

Daghestan

102 The region of Daghestan is now part of the Russian Federated Socialist Republic. Although many carpets are referred to as Daghestans, the one specific type that should be so-called is the distinctive prayer Daghestan. The mihrab arch on these prayer rugs is always six sided and the field of the mihrab is nearly always covered with a diamond-trellis pattern in which there are small, geometrically shaped polychrome flowers. The field is generally of an ivory colour. As far as can be established no Daghestan carpets have been made since the beginning of the Second World War. Although they are not of particularly outstanding quality they are nevertheless of considerable beauty and are keenly collected.

wineglass and serrated leaf border

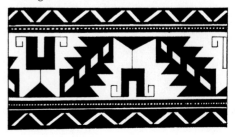

Daghestan prayer rug.
Caucasian, early 19th century.
Note the six-sided mihrab arch with the comb and signature.

Large Kuba carpet (detail).
Caucasian, 18th century.
22 ft × 8 ft 6 in.

Derbend

This type is only included since it is a frequently used name. Derbend carpets were made in the port of Derbent, capital of the Daghestan district, and closely followed the Daghestan design. Lewis wrote early this century that they were considered of little artistic interest and most authorities would agree with this judgement, although the fact that most of these are fairly old means that they have quite a high market value.

Erivan

This is a strictly twentieth-century type of carpet and indeed has only been made for about the last twenty years. It is named after the city of Erivan, a few miles from the Turkish border and about 150 miles from Tabriz in Persia. Although generally inferior copies of Shirvans, these carpets are, for modern pieces, remarkably well woven and are fairly colourful and decorative.

Kabistan (Kuba)

27, 103 Kabistan is a name which has probably caused and still causes more confusion than any other in the world of Oriental carpets, the problem being that nobody seems to be very certain exactly what a Kabistan is, although everybody agrees that it does exist. The town of Kuba in the Shirvan weaving district of southern Daghestan is the probable origin of these pieces, although there is now a specific type of carpet known as Kuba.

The problem arises because Bakus, Kubas, Daghestans and Kabistans frequently have the same designs thus making it almost impossible to differentiate them. In general the type of carpet which uses the ram's-horn design on the field is called a Kabistan. Although even with this, some authorities are in disagreement. If the piece does not show the distinctive pattern we have demonstrated to be characteristic of Bakus, Chi-Chis and Daghestans, and if the designs are more geometric than floral, then the carpet is either a Kabistan or a Kuba which, to the Russians, are synonymous.

A distinctive type of old Kuba is one with three large X patterns on the field, which certain experts refer to as Sejur. Another type is the dragon Kuba which, as its name implies, has figures of dragons woven into the field. Many authorities claim that it was at Kuba that the famous Dragon and the Phoenix carpet in Berlin was woven sometime in the fourteenth century. It should be noticed that modern carpets using Kabistan/Kuba designs are being woven at Ardebil in Persia; these use cotton for the warp and weft and are not of good quality.

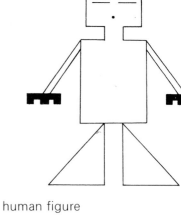
human figure

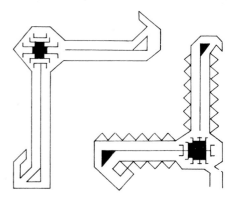
door-bolt key

104

Karabagh

Karabagh carpets are made in the southernmost area of the Caucasus, bordering on Persia. They are very floral in character, often having three or four large bouquets of flowers in Western European style on a central field and smaller floral sprays in a wide border. The main point of recognition for these pieces, however, is not the design but the field colour, frequently an extraordinarily vivid shade of magenta, which, being too strong for the Western market, was at the beginning of this century often changed by a chemical process to a dark black-brown. There are also some rare prayer rugs in which the mihrab usually has a central column with contrasting geometric patterns on either side and a square-arched top. Modern Karabaghs are made which keep to traditional designs but are usually of poor quality.

Kazak

106 The Kazak is one of the most famous types of Oriental carpet. Antique examples stopped being made around 1920 and should not be confused with the so-called Kazaks which the Russians have been marketing for the past ten years and which are poor-quality copies of a number of Caucasian designs, many of which are not Kazak within the traditional meaning of the word. The colours of a Kazak are usually bright reds, blues, greens and yellows, with a large amount of white. One of the most characteristic designs is the so-called sunburst which is in reality a schematised form of the Russian double-headed eagle. Carpets bearing this design are sometimes called Tcherkess. In general, Kazak carpets have a field filled with one or more large geometric medallions usually of rather eccentric shape (although the Greek cross and a design resembling the cross of Lorraine are not unusual). The border often bears a polychrome crab pattern on a white ground. Because of the bold, colourful surfaces, and also the extremely hard-wearing nature of the weave, which is coarse but dense, Kazaks are very popular with collectors.

Shirvan

107 This is a famous but problematic name. The carpets were woven in south Caucasia and marketed at Baku. None has apparently been made since the beginning of the Second World War, and the best examples date from the first two decades of this century or earlier. As we have said before, there is very little difference between Shirvans, Kabistans, Kubas and Daghestans, and any differences there may be are purely academic. As we have Jack Franses

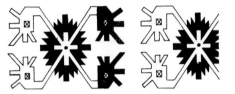

crab border

Shirvan tarantula

Kazak rug.
Caucasian, early 19th century.
The bold geometric motifs and the large areas
of white are characteristic of Kazak pieces.

says, 'Rugs are often labelled Shirvans for want of a better name'. Most authorities suggest that Shirvans are more floral in appearance than other Caucasian carpets but in general they would appear to be as geometric, if slightly more delicately so, as any other Caucasian piece.

Soumak

Soumaks are called after the city of Shemakha. They are also sometimes referred to as Cashmeres, apparently because their weave resembles that of cashmere shawls. They are nearly all more than sixty years old and the designs are much the same as Daghestans, Shirvans and other Caucasian carpets of the same group. They have, however, one great distinguishing feature: they are flat-woven and have no knotted pile, the only Oriental carpet thus made apart from the type known as kilim which we have already discussed. Some of the weft threads are wrapped around the warp in a kind of chain-stitch embroidery, making a decorative raised pattern. An additional design characteristic is the frequent appearance of small animals woven amongst the normal geometric medallions; they also always have a wave-scroll border.

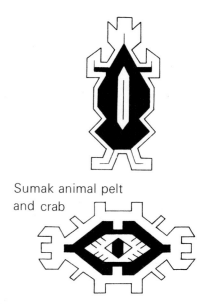

Sumak animal pelt and crab

Conclusion

The first point to be noted is that carpet-weaving to any great extent ceased in the Caucasus between thirty and fifty years ago and, although the Soviet Government has from time to time started the industry again, the vast majority of carpets produced in the last twenty years are of extremely poor quality. A discussion of Caucasian carpets, therefore, is almost solely concerned with antique pieces. The one exception is the Erivan.

The second point is that the designs of most old Caucasian carpets are so similar that, with the exceptions of Bakus, Chi-Chis and prayer Daghestans, most of which can be differentiated with reasonable success, the other names are perhaps of little practical value and should only concern the most fastidious of collectors.

Many Caucasian carpets use bold, almost primitive, geometric forms, some of which, as we have seen, are distinctive from one particular type to another, although it should be emphasised once again that the motifs one thinks are peculiar to one type will frequently appear on another. The exceptions to this are the Karabagh, which has rather crude floral designs, and the Shirvan, which, on little actual evidence, many authorities declare to be more floral than is usual for a Caucasian piece. Nearly all Caucasian carpets tend to be bright and colourful and it is rare to find them in large sizes.

6 Turkestan and Afghanistan

Turkestan was the name formerly given to the area, now a part of the U.S.S.R., which comprises the three Soviet States of Turkmen, Uzbek and Kazakh. The carpets from this area are generally known as Turkoman.

The eastern part, which is made up of the most easterly end of the huge State of Kazakh (not to be confused with the town of Kazak in the Caucasus) and the most westerly part of China, uses Samarkand as the chief market place and that city, like Bokhara to the west, has given its name to many of the carpets woven in its vicinity.

Turkoman carpets are also, as we shall see, woven in Afghanistan. Carpets made here almost always use the Persian knot, the exceptions being Yomuds. The distinguishing design of the Turkoman product is the red-brown field covered with orderly rows of small octagons; eastern pieces, however, are very Chinese in character.

The main carpet names are as follows:

Ersari	Salor Bokhara	Yomud Bokhara
Khiva Bokhara	Samarkand	
Pinde Bokhara	Tekke Bokhara	

Map of Turkestan and Afghanistan showing centres of carpet production.

Pinde Bokhara carpet.
Turkoman, early 19th century.

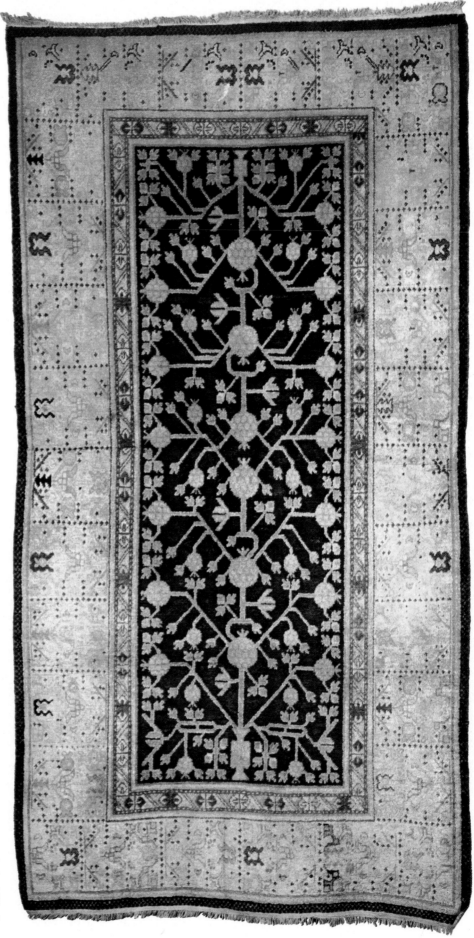

Samarkand carpet.
Turkoman, 19th century.
A pomegranate, symbol of plenty,
grows out of a small vase and
covers the central field.

We shall now examine each of these in detail, but first it should be pointed out that the correct term for any Turkoman prayer rug is a Hatchlie. Thus a Pinde Bokhara prayer rug is called a Pinde Hatchlie Bokhara.

Ersari

Some books refer to these carpets as Beshir Bokharas. They were woven by the Ersari tribes who lived on both sides of the Amu Darya (Oxus) river and who also inhabit Afghanistan. A typical pattern is a field with a zig-zag border following the outlines of a row of conjoined diamond medallions in the centre. Stylised tree patterns are also found in the centres. The predominant colour is dark red, with designs woven in reds, blues and yellows. The Persian knot is most frequently used although the Turkish is sometimes found. Most carpets, and also very attractive tent bags, are now woven by Ersari settlers in northern Afghanistan.

Khiva Bokhara

Khivas are also called Afghans, since in former times a sizeable quantity were woven in Afghanistan and today all are. The Persian knot is used, and the carpets are made in widely varying sizes although the large size examples are the best known and the most popular. The distinctive design consists of a deep rich red field which is woven with several rows of octagons, quartered and woven in two different colours. Even from a description such as this, it should be possible for the beginner to recognise a Khiva Bokhara immediately.

Pinde Bokhara

110 These exceptionally rare carpets were woven in the Turkmen district of Pinde. The prayer rugs have a red field and a distinctive design consisting of two narrow prayer niches separated by a wide horizontal bar usually woven with a large amount of white. From a distance the pattern looks like a large cross. They are amongst the most valuable of all Bokharas.

Salor Bokhara

These are made by the Salor tribe who used to inhabit the Merv oasis just north of the Afghan border. The carpets are of superb quality and of considerable rarity. The field is red, usually woven with two rows of octagons. These octagons can be distinguished by the fact that each large octagon has a small one within it and it is this interior one which is quartered; also the alternate interior sides of each octagon bear three trefoil flowers.

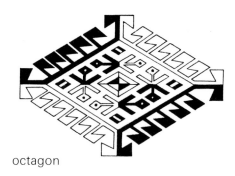
octagon

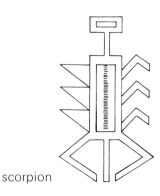
scorpion

camel

Samarkand

111 Woven in the vicinity of the central-Asian town of Samarkand, they are also marketed there. Although specialists can probably differentiate between the different types, such as Kotan, Yarkands, and Kansus (the latter in fact being a Chinese town) such distinctions are unnecessary for even the most serious collector. Almost all these carpets are very Chinese in appearance, having dragons, Chinese frets, roundels and other typical Chinese designs. Although antique examples are of fairly good quality, twentieth-century pieces are generally very poor. The Persian knot is used. The most typical designs are those with three large circular medallions in the field. The colours favoured are purple, green and yellow, which are now found attractively faded.

Samarkand octagon

Tekke Bokhara

114 This is one of the most famous Oriental carpet classifications. Tekkes are usually divided into two types, non-prayer rugs which are known as Royal Bokharas, and prayer rugs, called Princess Bokharas. In general they are amongst the most finely woven of all Oriental fabrics. The fields of both carpets are red; in the Royal Bokharas the field is woven with rows of distinctive elongated octagons, alternating with small diamonds, these octatons being joined horizontally and vertically with blue lines which quarter them. Princess Bokharas are, if anything, of an even more distinctive design. The main field is divided into four by the same upright mihrabs and separating crossbar as the Pinde design. The four quarters of the field are woven with bands of candlestick-shaped patterns in dark indigo blue which, once seen, can never be forgotten. Here again even a beginner can spot a Princess Bokhara. The Persian knot is used in all Tekkes.

Royal Bokhara octagon

Yomud Bokhara

Named after the large Yomud tribe which is to be found over most of central Asia, antique and semi-antique examples are still fairly freely available and are usually of good quality. There are two main designs; the one most often seen has the field divided into four by a Greek cross with small white octagons woven in the quarters; the second, and less common, has an all-over field of a diamond lattice with geometric medallions within each diamond. This is perhaps more of a Caucasian design and may have been woven by Yomud tribesmen who had wandered over in that direction. The fields of Yomuds are a deep rich red whilst either the Persian or the Turkish knot may be used.

Tekke Bokhara candlesticks

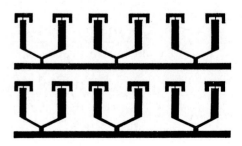

Tekke Bokhara.
Turkoman, late 18th century.
The kilim end, denoting the class of the weaver,
is only found in better-grade Tekkes.

An exceptionally large
Moghul carpet (detail).
Indian, from the time of the
Emperor Jahangir (1605-1627).
52 ft 4 in × 10 ft 8 in.

7 Pakistan, India and China

Although stylistically they perhaps belong in the previous chapter, the most important carpets woven in what is now Pakistan are discussed here for the sake of geographic unity. These are the Baluchistan carpets, named after the ancient state which was once located at the western side of the area that since 1947 has been called West Pakistan. They were in fact woven by the nomadic Baluche tribes, who also wandered over Persia and Afghanistan. They were almost always geometrically designed using the octagon and diamond medallions so frequently found in Turkoman fabrics. The colours, however, are darker and more sombre than is usual in Turkoman pieces and the Turkoman red is not so prevalent, large areas of dark blue being almost as common. The Persian knot was almost always used and still is in the modern Pakistan imitations.

There is at the moment a flourishing weaving industry in Pakistan producing two basic types of carpet: the Pakistanis and the Moris. Surprisingly, both types are of a fairly high quality although they are in a sense luxurious reproductions, having no national stylistic identities.

The Pakistani carpets closely follow Persian designs especially those of Tabriz and Kirman. The Moris are of exceptionally good quality and copy the designs of Tekke Bokharas; perhaps their most famous characteristic is that they are woven of Cashmere wool, giving them a smooth, velvety sheen. One cannot help regretting that the weavers of these pieces do not attempt to design the carpets, which have only been in production for less than twenty years, instead of copying an already famous pattern.

India has in the past produced some of the greatest 22, 39 carpets ever woven and is now second only to Persia as a carpet-weaving nation. The most important period was the late sixteenth and the early seventeenth centuries when under the patronage of the Moghul Emperor Akbar, the Indian contemporary of the Persian Shah Abbas, one

phoenix

116

of the greatest art patrons and collectors of all time, royal looms were established at Lahore under the supervision of Persian weavers. Very soon afterwards more looms were established at the royal capital of Agra and in other cities under Akbar's successors, Jahangir (1605–1627) and the great Shah Jahan (1628–1658), famous as the builder of the Taj Mahal. From the late seventeenth to the late nineteenth century very little carpet-weaving was done in India.

From about 1850 onwards, however, large factories, mostly run by English and latterly American companies, have been producing large quantities of carpets almost continuously. Many of these, although of good quality, are copies of French eighteenth-century designs and would appear to be most popular in America. They are marketed under a plethora of trade names. Below is a short list of some of the most important Indian carpets:

Agra   Indo-Saruk   Kandahar   Lahore

We shall now examine each of these in detail.

Agra

These have not been made for about fifty years. When one refers to Agra carpets, which are usually in very large sizes, one means those woven in Agra Fort in the second half of the nineteenth century. Their designs are mainly Persian inspired but with colours such as plum, cream, sea-green, scarlet, black and yellow. They are now of some rarity and are eagerly collected; they are usually finely knotted and very hard-wearing.

Agra border motif

Indo-Saruk

Like the Agras, these carpets have not been woven for many years and are normally in large sizes. As their name implies, they were largely based upon early twentieth-century Persian Saruk carpets and, as far as the designs were concerned, they usually had a large rose-coloured field woven with floral patterns.

Kandahar

Pre-Second World War Kandahar carpets were poor-quality copies of Persian designs similar in style to Agras. Today the name is used as a trade description for one of the many similar kinds of large carpet woven to French eighteenth-century Savonnerie designs. Indo-French carpets of this type have in fact been woven in India since the early eighteenth century, the French having established workshops in the town of Pondicherri when they purchased it in 1702. The Kandahar, like other Indo-

Large Moghul carpet (detail).
Indian, 18th century.
27 ft 5 in × 10 ft.

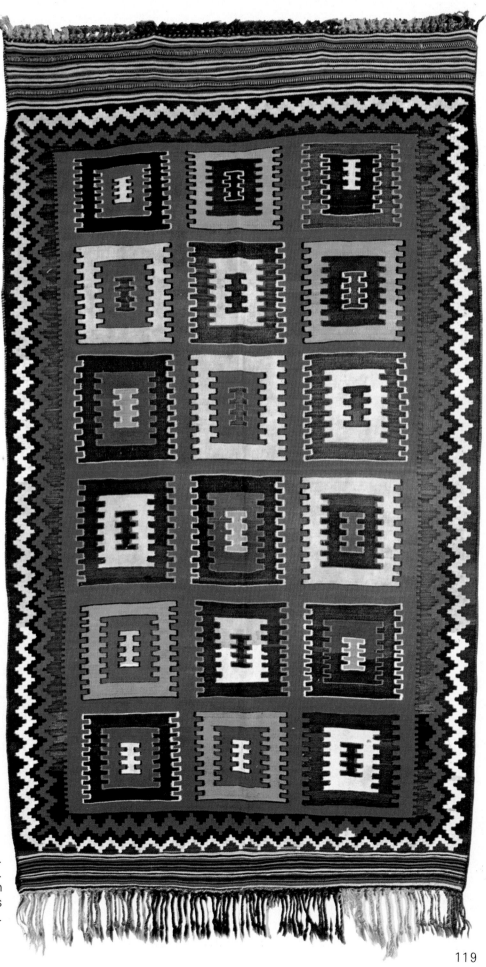

Shiraz kilim.
Persian, 19th century.
Woven in wool and hair with
some of the white areas
in cotton.

French carpets, such as the so-called jewel of Kashmir carpets which are pileless, are woven in large British- and American-owned factories. They are of fairly good weave and are hard wearing.

Lahore

These carpets, woven in the sixteenth and seventeenth centuries on the royal Moghul looms, are considered amongst the greatest carpets ever made; they are often referred to as Indo-Isfahans since they closely follow the Isfahan floral designs (it is probable that the first weavers at Lahore, who were brought from Persia by the Emperor Akbar, came from Isfahan). One of the finest of these carpets, woven in the second decade of the seventeenth century, is the Girdler's carpet which hangs in the Gird-ler's Hall in the city of London. This is one of several pieces of this kind and was imported into England soon after it was made. Carpets from this period are virtually unknown outside museums and, if they ever appeared on the market, would be of the greatest value.

China

30 No Chinese carpets earlier than the late Ming dynasty of the mid seventeenth century seem to have survived, although it seems certain that in a country with such an ancient civilisation, carpets were woven long before then. The few Ming carpets that have come down to us are generally of the same type with a large field of a single colour, usually a vivid pale blue or rich tan. On this field would be woven one or two figures, often animals, whilst there was a fret-work border.

From the beginning of the eighteenth century up to the mid nineteenth, Persian influence steadily grew in the Chinese carpet-weaving industry and floral patterns predominate. After the mid nineteenth century, Chinese designs increasingly came under the influence of the European and American markets, which had their own ideas about what a Chinese carpet should look like. This was a period when very obvious Chinese motifs, dragons, cranes, bats and objects resembling archaic Chinese bronzes, appeared together with the ubiquitous Chinese-fret design and the pao-shau-hai-shui pattern resembling overlapping waves.

In the present century Chinese weavers, like Indians, have tended to favour the French Savonnerie designs and all the carpets are chemically washed to give the pile a silky appearance. Few pieces now reach the Western market and are not, in general, very highly regarded.

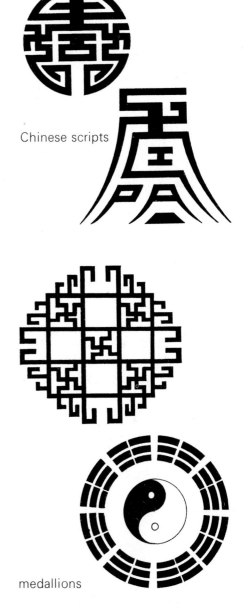

Chinese scripts

medallions

8 Miscellaneous Carpets

Before moving on to the section concerned with the mechanics of buying, selling, and maintaining carpets, we should discuss the remaining types of Oriental carpet and the countries which produce carpets in small quantities. Kilims, the weft-face carpets which are woven throughout the Middle East, we have dealt with earlier.

119

The countries and areas we have covered in the main body of this book are those from which approximately ninety-eight percent of all Oriental carpets originate. Other countries which should be mentioned for the sake of completeness are Egypt, Morocco, Nepal and Tibet. The last two mentioned can be covered in a few words; Nepalese pieces are woven in the Himalayas, and the designs, usually dragons, on a plain yellow ground are Chinese. The same applies to Tibetan pieces.

122

Egypt, like China, had one of the most ancient civilisations and it is known from the evidence of tomb paintings that weaving was an established occupation there some 2000 years or more before Christ. The great period of Egyptian carpets, however, was between roughly 1500 and 1700 when the country was part of the Turkish Ottoman Empire. Very fine carpets were woven in Cairo imitating the designs of Damascene metal work, as well as fine copies of famous Persian designs; these latter pieces frequently had silk warps and wefts (as cotton was unknown in Egypt before the mid eighteenth century). Today the industry is virtually non-existent.

123

Morocco also became part of the Ottoman Empire in the early sixteenth century; a few carpets of the same type as those woven in Egypt were produced there. There are virtually none of these known today and the only Moroccan carpets that survive in any quantity are the coarse, geometrically designed and brightly coloured pieces woven in the nineteenth century.

The Japanese carpet industry is less than twenty years old. Strangely enough, they too, like the Indians and the Chinese, have chosen to copy French Savonnerie designs, presumably influenced by the American market, which is their only customer. These carpets are large, heavy, finely woven and the designs are often carved into the pile in relief (as was done with some eighteenth-century Indian carpets). They are also exorbitantly priced.

Tibetan saddle cloth.
18th century.
The motifs are typically Chinese;
the four holes are for saddle straps.

Rare Cairo rug.
Egyptian, 16th century.

122

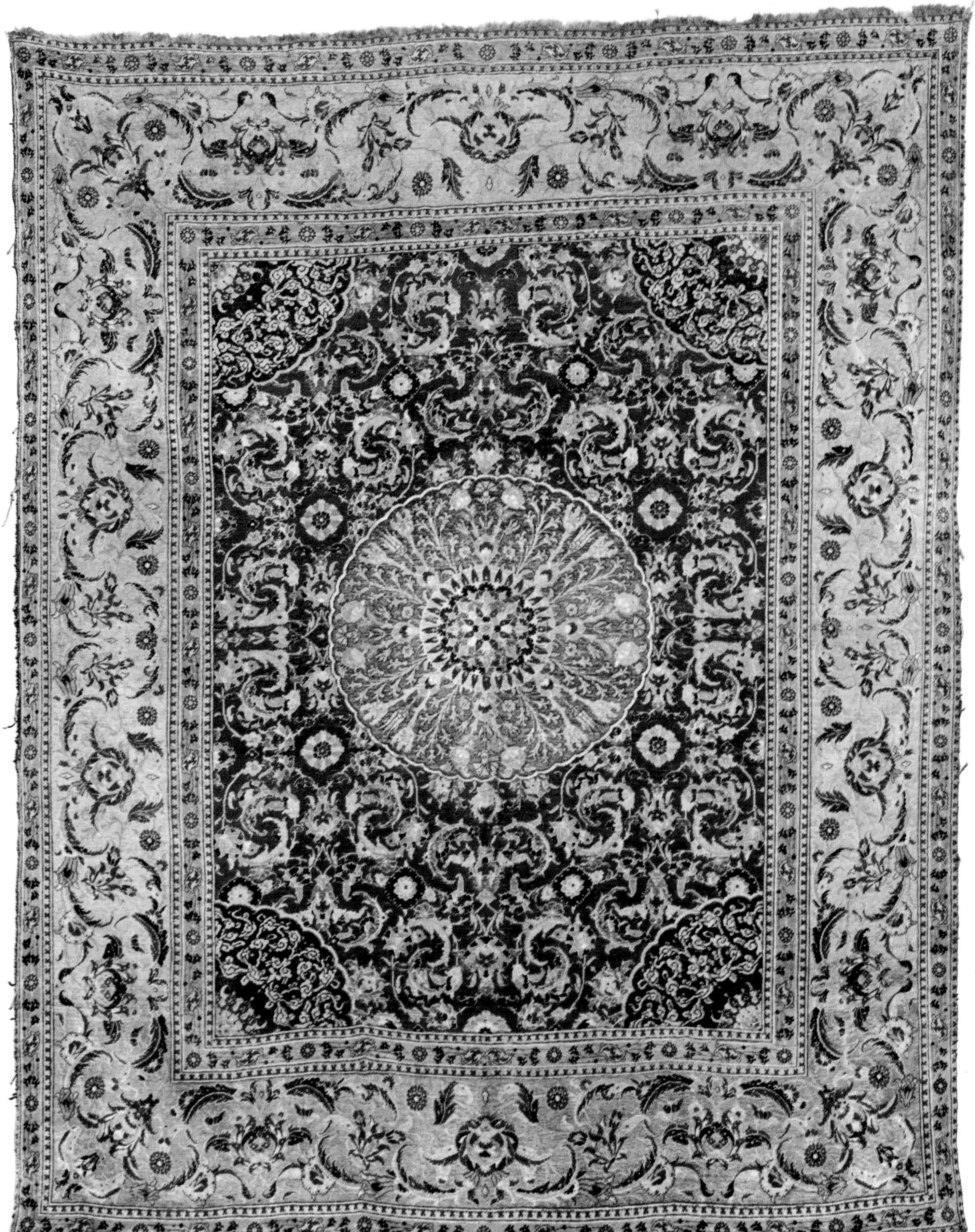

9 Buying, Selling, Maintaining

There are two basic ways of buying and selling Oriental carpets, one is through a dealer, the other at auction. In both cases, the rules to be followed are the same, whether you are, to use Jacobsen's phrase, 'a hobbyiest or a seeker of floor coverings'. The qualities which go to make one piece more valuable than another are ones which are immediately apparent to anyone with commonsense. The age of the carpet, its condition, its place of origin and the quality of the weaving are the four main criteria which have to be assessed. In this respect carpets are like books—an old book is not necessarily valuable in itself, it must be a combination of being the right book by the right author published at the right time and in the right condition.

The advantage of a good dealer over the auction house is that the buyer is offered a wide choice of carpets which have been restored to the best possible condition and he can learn exactly the extent of such restoration whilst getting to know at the same time a carpet's exact state of preservation. In an auction sale, carpets are sold with all errors or imperfections unnoted although at major salerooms such as Sotheby's and Christie's in London, or Parke-Bernet in New York, major restorations will be noted and experts are on hand to advise clients.

To buy carpets at auction, however, requires a greater degree of expertise than to buy from a good dealer. You will in a saleroom, for instance, notice people taking a corner of a carpet and twisting it. If a dry cracking sound results, then the foundation threads have rotted and will in time disintegrate. When buying from a reputable dealer, this kind of preliminary testing will already have been done by experts and any repairs necessary will have been carried out.

It should be said, however, that the chance of purchasing important antique pieces is far greater in a saleroom, given that you are prepared to pay anything from £5,000 ($12,000) upwards. A dealer is far more likely to have a large stock of semi-antique and modern pieces at prices far below this sum although there are, of course, some dealers who keep a small stock of important antique pieces. A reputable dealer will also always be prepared to act as an agent and advisor to clients wishing to purchase at auction.

In selling a carpet, the owner must bear in mind how he came by the piece he wishes to sell and the length of time it has been in his possession. If treated with respect, fine antique carpets will wear for decades, not to mention centuries. A carpet purchased from a good dealer can usually be resold to him within a few years and provided that it has been well cared for the seller should realise a good profit. Carpets, like most other types of art, have gone up in value considerably in the last twenty years, even in the last ten years. Our advice with regard to good antique pieces is to sell them in a reputable auction house such as the ones we have mentioned above. By selling in a public auction, the client is given the advantage of the publicity his piece will receive in a catalogue which will be distributed to all leading collectors and dealers throughout the world. Although the number of serious collectors of valuable antique pieces is small, a piece sold in this way will at least attract the greatest attention and, it is hoped, the most competition.

Caring for Oriental carpets is something which requires skill and expertise. To borrow another quaint phrase from an American writer, Lewis, 'Oriental rugs cannot be handled and beaten like the domestic without serious injury'. Ignoring the visions of outraged and tearful chambermaids this conjures up, its message is one to be remembered. It is doubtful whether anyone walks on really antique pieces any more and in any case it should be noted that the shoes were always removed before prayer rugs were walked upon.

Carpets naturally get grit and dirt in their pile which, if it is not regularly removed, will have an abrasive action with, eventually, disastrous consequences. Oriental carpets should be swept, preferably with an electric carpet sweeper, both on the front and back; they should never be beaten. Once a year, they should be examined by an expert to see if any serious restorations are needed or if they need washing. And remember that carpets, like hats, should never be brushed against the pile, as this only pushes the dirt deeper into the fabric. If an Oriental carpet is regularly examined, cleaned and generally treated with respect, there is no reason, given that it is of good quality, why it should not go on giving as much pleasure far into the future as it has done for so many centuries past.

CARPET DEALERS
The following is a list of the most important Oriental carpet specialists in London and New York City. Any competent antique directory will give the names of dealers in other cities and countries.

LONDON
A. Arditti
12B Berkeley Street, W1.
Benardout & Benardout
7 Thurloe Place, S.W.7.
Robert Frances & Son
5 Nugent Terrace, N.W. 8.
Frances of Piccadilly Ltd.
169 Piccadilly, London W.1.
S. Franses (Carpets) Ltd.
71–3 Knightsbridge, S.W.1.
J. Haim & Co.
31 Brook Street, W.1.
C. John
70 South Audley Street, W.1.
Alexander Juran & Co.
74 New Bond Street, W.1.
Perez (London) Ltd.
112 Brompton Road, S.W.3.
Persian Carpet Galleries
152 Brompton Road, S.W.3.
Pontremoli Ltd.
11 Spring Street, W.2.
Vigo-Sternberg Gallery Ltd.
6A Vigo Street, W.1.

NEW YORK CITY
Beshar's
63 East 52nd Street, N.Y. 10022
Beshir Galleries
1125 Madison Avenue, N.Y. 10028
Vojtech Blau
980 Madison Avenue, N.Y. 10021
Archie Chamalian
785 Madison Avenue, N.Y. 10021
J. H. Dildarian Inc.
762 Madison Avenue, N.Y. 10021
Oskan Harootunian & Sons Inc.
51 East 54th Street, N.Y. 10022
Mayorkas Brothers
843 Madison Avenue, N.Y. 10021
M. Michaelbard
306 East 61st Street, N.Y. 10021
A. Morjikian Co.
339 East 60th Street, N.Y. 10022

Acknowledgements

I should firstly like to express my gratitude to Charles Walford of the Furniture Department at Sotheby's. He has advised me during all stages of this book and read the manuscript on completion, making numerous corrections and additions. All errors that have remained, however, are purely my responsibility.

I must also thank Miss Anne Tillard of Sotheby's who in her own time and with amazing efficiency and speed typed the final draft from my illegible manuscript.

The photographs on the front jacket and pages 20, 30, 51, 54, 62, 70, 71, 91, 102, 106, 107, 108, 110, 111, 114, 119, 122 are reproduced by courtesy of Benardout and Benardout, London.

SOURCES OF PHOTOGRAPHS
Fratelli Fabbri Editori, Milan pp. 14, 18, 23, 35, 46
Fogg Art Museum, Harvard University, Cambridge, Mass. p. 11
Hamlyn Group Picture Library – Hawkley Studio Associates, front jacket, pp. 20, 30, 51, 54, 62, 70, 71, 91, 102, 106, 107, 110, 111, 114, 119, 122
Hamlyn Group Picture Library – M. Holford p. 38
Keystone Press Agency Ltd., London p. 125
McGraw-Hill Book Company, New York p. 2
Metropolitan Museum of Art, New York pp. 47, 83
Museum of Fine Arts, Boston p. 22
National Portrait Gallery, London p. 6
Österreichisches Museum für angewandte Kunst, Vienna pp. 19, 31
Sotheby and Co., London pp. 15, 26, 27, 34, 39, 42, 43, 50, 55, 58, 59, 63, 66, 67, 74, 75, 78, 79, 82, 86, 87, 90, 94, 95, 98, 99, 103, 115, 118, 123, back jacket
Weidenfeld and Nicolson Ltd., London p. 10

Index